PRICING: THE THIRD BUSINESS SKILL

Pricing: The Third Business Skill

PRINCIPLES OF PRICE MANAGEMENT

Ernst-Jan Bouter

© 2013 FirstPrice B.V., Loenen aan de Vecht, The Netherlands

ISBN 978-90-820693-0-3

Original title: *Pricing: de derde business skill. Principes van prijsmanagement*
Translation: Erwin Postma, Málaga, Spain
Cover design: Griet Van Haute, Gent, Belgium
Cover illustration: Gerrit Adriaensz. Berckheyde, *View of the 'Golden Bend' in Herengracht, Amsterdam, 1671-1672.* Photo © Rijksmuseum, Amsterdam
Photo author: Geert Linssen, Loenen aan de Vecht
Typography: Sander Pinkse Boekproductie, Amsterdam
Proof correction: Kate Elliott, Rooksbridge, UK
Editing and production: Wardy Poelstra, Amsterdam

Contents

Preface

An important part of the origins of modern capitalism can be traced back to the Golden Age of the Dutch Republic. In 1602, the *Vereenigde Oostindische Compagnie* (Dutch East India Company) was established. The VOC was the first company in history to raise capital by issuing stock, which led to the foundation of the world's first stock exchange. Global trade, on an until then unprecedented scale, was the source of the vast wealth of Amsterdam's merchants. The Dutch preferred trade at attractive prices to conquering foreign lands as a way of amassing wealth. The richest of Amsterdam's merchants lived in the so-called Golden Bend of the Herengracht canal. The cover of this book shows the nearly completed Golden Bend, as depicted by Gerrit Adriaensz Berckheyde in 1671-72.

This book is about setting prices for customers in a free capitalist economy, where price is a tool entrepreneurs can use to achieve their goals. This book, too, originated in the Netherlands. For you as the reader I hope this book will be a "golden bend" leading to the business success that can help you fulfill your dreams.

Naturally, it is impossible to write a book that is the product of a career without the help and encouragement of many. I owe a great debt of gratitude to all co-workers and clients I have had the privilege of working with at several companies and as an independent consultant. I am grateful for what I was able to learn from them and the time I got to spend with them.

I would like to thank Boet, Bert, and Marc for their exceptional encouragement, as for many years they kept urging me to write this book. Hans, Herman, Corinne, Leendert, Cora, and Henriëtte have been a great support to me by reviewing and commenting on the draft material I produced. Wardy, Erwin, Sander, Griet, Kate, and Milan worked meticulously in helping me turn my scribblings into a professional publication. And finally, my family, Sophie, Tobias, Bente, and Henriëtte, has shown great flexibility and tolerance of the constant switching between the highly demanding projects of a pricing manager and the peace and quiet of a writer.

Ernst-Jan
Loenen aan de Vecht (NL)
April 27th, 2013

Introduction

CHAPTER 1

The third business skill

1.1 Entrepreneurship

Entrepreneurs are the driving force behind the prosperity of their enterprises, and both personal skills and business acumen are essential success factors. When it comes to business skills, two archetypes are often used to define what makes an entrepreneur an entrepreneur: "the inventor" and "the salesman".

1.1.1 THE FIRST BUSINESS SKILL (THE INVENTOR)

The first business skill is the ability to create value and produce goods or services. Bill Gates managed to provide IBM with an operating system for its PCs almost overnight, setting Microsoft on its way toward global dominance.

The power of creation reflects positively on entrepreneurs' public image. Where would we be today without the inventions of Thomas Edison, Nikola Tesla, Bill Gates, Steve Jobs, Steve Wozniak, Larry Page, Sergey Brin, Mark Zuckerberg[*] and all those other creative business brains of our time?

---

[*] These are the product developers from the early days of General Electric, Westinghouse, Microsoft, Apple, Google, and Facebook respectively

As companies grow and departments gain shape, knowledge generated by the creation process is harnessed by R&D and product management, and applied in operations and production. A large number of the available resources go into this first business skill. The aim is to efficiently produce and provide good products.

1.1.2 THE SECOND BUSINESS SKILL (THE SALESMAN)

The second business skill is the ability to sell products or services. Entrepreneurs drive progress by improving sales methods for the benefit of both buyers and sellers. Jeff Bezos, Michael Dell, Pierre Omidyar[*], to name but a few, pioneered sales when they started selling physical goods online on a major scale. All services and products sold under British entrepreneur Stelios Haji-Ioannou's[†] 'Easy' brand are, as the name suggests, easy to order and use by anyone who is fed up with other providers' poor service.

The second business skill is the domain of commerce, the realm in which sales and marketing departments operate. The extent of resources allocated to these activities differs per industry and per business model, while those in charge of commercial operations tend to be firmly rooted in the highest echelons of a company.

The two business skills are represented by two prototypes of entrepreneurs. The inventor turns a great idea into reality, and has something unique to offer consumers. The salesman can sell anything, even "ice to Eskimos". An often recurring phenomenon is that of an inventor and a sales professional setting up a company together.

1.2 Pricing: the third business skill

Prevailing views on entrepreneurship claim that all the ingredients for business success are present if you know what you have to offer and how to make it (skill 1) and also manage to sell it (skill 2).

---

[*] Founders of Amazon, Dell, and E-bay respectively
[†] Founder of easyJet and other companies, such as easyHotel

This book focuses on the *third business skill,* on *pricing*: setting and asking the right price in order to hit business targets. This often neglected skill is indispensable for sustained success. Getting the pricing right will ensure you obtain enough revenue from those unique products and services you are selling so well.

For Google, it was the third business skill that propelled the breakthrough of a start-up with superior search technology (skill 1) that eventually became one of the most high-profile companies in the first decade of the 21st century. A revenue model that aligned advertising rates with users' searches (skill 3) was the starting point of Google's growth. Like no other company, Google understands the importance of a sound pricing strategy. Also for services such as YouTube, Google+, and Docs, Google takes the time to develop the right revenue model. In doing so, Google relies on the services of specialist pricing managers.

The third business skill enables entrepreneurs and CEOs to realize growth and make the most of their company's potential. Yet, the majority of companies still largely overlook pricing in their organizational set-up. Where the first two business skills are well established in any company in the form of R&D, production, marketing, and sales departments, pricing's place in companies' departmental line-up is often less clearly defined. Only a very few companies have a Chief Pricing Officer.[1] Responsibility for pricing tends to be scattered over different departments, resulting in suboptimal coordination of pricing.

1.3 Target readership and objective

Good pricing governance starts with the CEO. He or she understands what his or her company makes and how to sell it. The CEO needs the same level of understanding of pricing.

Ideally, the CEO himself also holds the position of Chief Pricing Officer, as did, each in his own way, Steve Jobs,[2] Sam Walton[3] and Albert Heijn.[4] Making good pricing decisions requires vision, a customer perspective, and knowledge of all parts of the company. Failing a CEO who doubles up as a pricing chief, a dedicated Chief Pricing Officer working alongside the CEO can bring the kind of focus on pricing that the business requires.

This book sets out to raise awareness of the importance and workings of the pricing function among entrepreneurs, CEOs, and other stakeholders. Insights presented in this book will enable the reader to evaluate pricing strategies, revenue models, research methods, and the organization of the pricing function.

After reading this book, you will be able to assess to what extent your company masters the third business skill and where it needs to further hone this skill. Marketing, sales, and finance professionals will find the insights acquired through this book very helpful in their day-to-day activities. Collaboration across pricing processes will improve. And they will also acquire better understanding of the needs of pricing specialists.

1.4 Structure of this book

The next chapter (Ch.2) will focus on "the pricing perspective". This perspective needs further development, because otherwise opportunities that present themselves in day-to-day business will go begging.

The three parts following this introduction will address this book's central themes:
- The Art of Pricing (why?)
- The Science of Pricing (what?)
- The Execution of Pricing (how?)

"The Art of Pricing" covers the strategy underlying pricing and revenue models. We will show that there are more roads that lead to Rome. And we will identify twelve price drivers, each with its own impact on pricing. Together these form the building blocks of a pricing strategy.

"The Science of Pricing" implements the pricing strategy, defining the optimum price point based on data analysis ("to measure is to know"). We will draw on three layers of knowledge of price sensitivity, i.e., expert judgment (1), implicit measurement (2), and explicit measurement (3). Optimum use of these three layers depends on the outcome and costs of the analyses.

The final part is entitled "The Execution of Pricing". The pricing process churns out prices for primary processes to use, such as sales, billing, and reporting. We will track the steps of this process on three process levels: strategic, tactical, and operational.

We will go into the organization of pricing efforts and the distribution of tasks and responsibilities within the company. And finally, we will discuss change management aspects that play a role in aspiring to boost pricing performance.

CHAPTER 2

The pricing perspective

2.1 Perspective

Perspective defines what you see and what you don't see. People observe things as they appear to them in their day-to-day lives. For example, media convey those events they consider the most important and thereby shape the perspective of the audience. Their readers and viewers process news items as they are served up to them.

In a similar way, items on the agenda of a company's board shape the perspective of middle managers and employees. Price is rarely an item on that agenda, which is down to the fact that no one on the board has direct and undivided responsibility for pricing. The commercial director is responsible for sales and revenue. The financial director's focus is on accounts and reports, as well as on major financial transactions. The operational director makes sure production is efficient. And the CEO fulfils a coordinating role and is the public face of the company.

Broken up into several pieces, the pricing policy comes under the competency of the commercial, managing, financial, and operational directors. Each director only sees a piece of the pricing puzzle, and the consequences of suboptimal prices often go unnoticed. Pricing is considered a *given*, and not a critical *decision*; the price is exogenous instead of endogenous.

The result is an underdeveloped perspective on pricing. Scant heed paid to pricing matters at board level leads to pricing decisions being sometimes made almost casually, with the decision-making process largely hidden from view, and only the end product, i.e., prices, reaching the desks of managers and employees.

Organization of the pricing function is barely explicit and almost always suboptimal. Every echelon of management rates projects in other areas more highly. These prioritized activities can therefore count on greater attention, perpetuating the status quo of poor pricing awareness.

Pricing's invisibility is in stark contrast to the opportunities better pricing offers. Prices have a major impact on financial results. A study involving 2,463 companies[5] showed that a 1% improvement in price yields an average boost to profits of 11%, trumping both a sales volume increase and reduction of fixed or variable costs in terms of impact on profit (also refer to Figure 1). A price improvement will, after all, raise revenue but not costs. This creates a lever effect on operating profits, which due to stagnant costs will increase by the same amount as revenue (also refer to Figure 2).

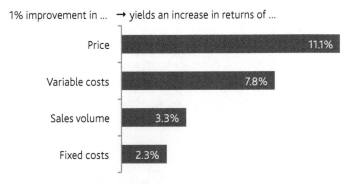

1% improvement in ... → yields an increase in returns of ...

Price	11.1%
Variable costs	7.8%
Sales volume	3.3%
Fixed costs	2.3%

Figure 1 Price improvement has the greatest impact (also refer to Marn and Rosiello, 1992)

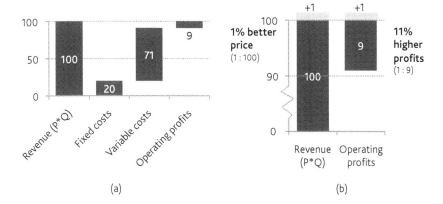

Figure 2 Lever effect of price (also refer to Marn and Rosiello, 1992):
(a) averages of costs and profit as a percentage of revenue emerging from the survey
(b) lever effect of a price improvement of 1%. A 1% better price generates 1% more revenue
(1:100). Revenue rises from 100 to 101. Costs remain unchanged. *Profit* will consequently also
go up by 1, i.e., from 9 to 10. This is an 11% profit increase (11% = 1:9)

The outcome will be different from one company to the next, as the ratio of fixed to variable costs will not be the same in every company. Current profit levels condition the relative impact of improvements. However, the impact of price is *always* greater than that of the other three profit drivers, i.e., sales volume, fixed costs, and variable costs.

These kinds of studies have meanwhile caught the attention of company directors, partly through the influence of boardroom advisors who have discovered the benefits of pricing. And yet it often turns out to be hard to achieve improvements. Most companies lack a broadly shared idea of what is needed for better pricing. This is due to a lack of vision on pricing and inadequate expertise. In the words of former soccer great Johan Cruijff: "You won't see it until you've figured it out".[6] And that is precisely what this book intends to do, help you "figure out" pricing.

This chapter will focus on the consequences of the underdeveloped perspective on pricing, showing how important that perspective is. In the following chapters, this book will embark on a step-by-step journey toward full understanding of the pricing function that will help companies bring their perspective on pricing into focus.

2.2 Conventions of pricing

2.2.1 TWO POPULAR CRITERIA

Research performed in developed and emerging economies has shown that most companies go by two criteria in setting the price for their products or services: cost price and market price.[7] This leads to two pricing methods that are referred to as "cost-plus" pricing and "competitive" pricing.

The popularity of these two criteria is striking, as pricing experts have pointed out that they do not lead to optimum prices.[8] From Chapter 3 of part I ("Art of Pricing") onward, we will explore alternatives and improvements. This section, however, will first focus on cost-plus and competitive pricing, on how they work, what the drawbacks are, and why they are so popular.

2.2.2 COST-PLUS PRICING

Cost price as a basis for selling price
Under the cost price principle, selling price equals average cost price plus profit mark-up, whereby cost price is calculated by dividing total costs by sales volume. The extent of the profit mark-up is derived from internal return requirements, historic conventions, or generally accepted practices in the industry.

The calculation is therefore as follows:

Selling price   = average cost price × (1 + % profit mark-up)

Average cost price = total costs / sales volume

Reasons for popularity
Cost-plus pricing gets its appeal from three qualities that this method is generally believed to have: simplicity, fairness, and prudence. [9] Implementing this principle seems *simple*, as it comprises a straightforward calculation that uses input that is readily available internally. Using a fixed profit mark-up is considered to be a *fair* way of recoup-

ing costs and putting a "justifiable" part aside for future investments. And its *prudence* lies in the conviction that costs are "always covered" this way.

The ostensible advantages of simplicity, fairness, and prudence are, however, based on fallacies. By exposing these fallacies, we will open new avenues toward a better pricing strategy.

1. Nontransparent

The alleged *simplicity* of cost-plus pricing only stands up when you take the sales volume forecast and extent of the profit mark-up as read. If you were to explore these factors further, links would be revealed between sales volume, market circumstances, competitiveness, profit mark-up, and pricing.

Cost-plus pricing hides the market's supply and demand forces behind the sales forecast and profit mark-up variables, obscuring the company's view of the reality of the customer and the market. This is what makes the pricing analysis *nontransparent*. Cost-plus pricing analyses neither what prices customers would be willing to pay, nor which product features really matter to customers and drive them to choose your product over that of your competitors.

2. Unfair

The *fairness* of cost-plus pricing is relative. The profit mark-up is in itself a subjective choice. And other components of the cost calculation require further subjective choices regarding, for example, volumes. Aside from that, it is *unfair* to withhold certain products from people only because the average *total* cost price is beyond their purchasing reach, when they would be able to afford a price that is higher than the *variable* cost price. For example: the price of medication can be lower in the Third World after fixed costs that went into R&D investments have been recovered in the First World. Cheap tickets for flights will remain available to tourists as long as the airline can cover the fixed costs of maintaining the route by selling expensive tickets to business travelers, who are willing to pay a premium for better service and greater comfort.

And finally, is it really unfair to provide consumers with free search engines online and free software? Users are satisfied with the service Facebook offers, but they are not paying anything to cover Facebook's costs.

3. Reckless

Prudence too is a quality that has been erroneously ascribed to cost-plus pricing. After all, this prudence depends heavily on the forecasts of total costs and sales volume being correct. Failure to live up to forecast sales volumes will put pressure on profits. This often prompts a company to start giving discounts, which will eat away at the profit margins that the company put on the selling price as a measure of prudence. Besides, this sends a signal to customers, as well as sales staff, that the price was too high initially. Customers will expect another discount next year, even when they were satisfied with the product.

We are seeing that this method leads to *reckless* behavior, which can run companies into financial difficulty as they chase false truths. The only genuine truth a company can go by is confirmation of supplied value. Profitable prices that reflect the value for customers provide that confirmation: the proof of the pudding is in the price.

Subjectivity

It is important to realize that average cost is a subjective factor,[10] because calculating average cost requires assumptions in three areas:
1. total costs
2. sales volume
3. profit mark-up

Total costs are made up of direct and indirect costs. Indirect costs include overheads, R&D investments, production facility costs, and sales channel expenses. To a certain extent, indirect costs are allocated to products arbitrarily. They depend on, among other things, considerations of volume, value, production capacity, and tax implications. And then there is also the distinction between fixed and variable costs. The way investments are written down influences the cost calculation.

The *sales volume* that is relevant for pricing is the sales volume in the future. This value will be unknown at the moment costs are calculated: it is based on estimation. And the *profit mark-up*, finally, is by definition also a subjective choice.

Besides assumptions in the three aforementioned areas, the source of the data used is also chosen subjectively. This data is obtained either from accounts based on the past (actual costing), or from the budget or business plan based on a forecast (cost estimate). Ideally, cost estimates and actual costs are aligned. A cost estimate will then be *calibrated* on the level of products, services, and subcomponents based on the actual costs. In practice, however, this kind of alignment is rarely performed as a structural and transparent activity that adheres to fixed procedures.

2.2.3 COMPETITIVE PRICING

Market price principle

The market price principle synchronizes the selling price with the price competitors charge. Salespeople want prices that are in line with those of the competition. "Because whenever a customer can choose between my product and someone else's product that costs 10% less, a customer will naturally always go for the competitor's product."

Drawbacks

This reasoning seems legitimate. Customers are drawn to lower prices. But price is not the only thing that differentiates you from your competitors. This book will explore the possibility of improving selling prices through differentiation. Competitive or me-too pricing is a form of laziness.[11] "Price" is often quoted as the reason for losing business. But in most cases, there is a significant lack of insight into the needs of the customer and the actual weight of the price in customers' acquisition decisions. Generally, price only has a share of under 50% in consumers' and companies' buying decisions. Other factors combined (such as quality, service, brand and terms of supply) are at least equally important.

Failure to recognize market dynamics and supply factors is another risk users of the competitive pricing method expose themselves to. Price cuts are tempting if sales and market share are only dependent on price and market prices are a given. However, competitors will match your price cuts, especially when the entire industry is caught up in the competitive pricing paradigm. A downward spiral is easily sparked, but the consequences will reverberate for years in the form of a marginally performing industry.

Defining "the" market price is not as easy as it seems. It requires thorough understanding of who your immediate competitors are: your so-called peer group. And it is also important to keep track of competitors' prices using an explicit and structural process. In practice, these kinds of activities are often only performed irregularly and inconsistently.

2.2.4 FROM TUNNEL VISION TO AN INTEGRATED APPROACH

The problems of cost-plus and competitive pricing are the result of tunnel vision. Although costs are a relevant benchmark in assessing the impact of price on a company's financial health, and a cost analysis will therefore provide the input needed for pricing, cost is not the only or even the dominant driver.

Prices competitors charge for a certain product give consumers a rough idea of what the normal price is for that kind of product. Market price is consequently an adequate starting point in setting a price, but you can only add value by being different. You can express that in your price through, for example, price customization, price communication, or by boosting returns on relationships with customers, stakeholders and/or users through pricing.

2.3 Analysis and execution

2.3.1 A STRATEGY IS ONLY AS GOOD AS ITS IMPLEMENTATION

An effective pricing strategy that uses sound criteria to set prices will be worthless if it is poorly executed. In practice, many problems will arise as a result of, for example, inadequate analyses and research methods, poorly trained staff, a divided organization and/or processes that eventually lead to incorrect, incomplete, or inefficient implementation of decisions.

This section will focus on problems in the area of analysis and execution, presenting examples of instances where quality and accuracy are at issue, and looking at the importance of speed, customer focus, training, and quality control.

2.3.2 QUALITY AND ACCURACY

Suboptimal pricing often goes hand in hand with inadequate tooling and insufficient attention to detail in the implementation. Such negligence has a major impact. A calculation error of 5% in pricing is sometimes spotted late, while it can cut annual profits by half. And yet it is understandable that underlying calculations and tooling fall short, when you consider that operations and training simply lack a pricing perspective. Below you will find a few examples of situations where poor quality and inaccuracy of prices cause problems.

Manual data processing
Changes to a hardware manufacturer's price list have led to numerous incorrect invoices to importers. An inquiry ordered by the board reveals that marketing managers are entering price changes manually. They do this separately in two systems, the price list in MS Excel and in the ERP system. They receive no support from IT.

The price list is the basis for communication with importers and customers. It contains tens of thousands of prices for products and parts in dozens of countries, sales channels, and currencies. Invoices are sent from the ERP system. Managers populate the tables in both systems manually, entry by entry, without verifying the correctness of the input. Errors in the systems are only corrected when reported by importers.

A salesman's "win price"
A successful business service provider has a pricing process that involves comparisons of market prices, cost prices, and margins. When drafting an offer, every salesman estimates the "win price": the price that will land him the contract. Salesmen base their estimate on several offers from the past year, feedback from customers, and prices that have landed their or other companies contracts in the past.

Finance subsequently calculates how much profit this price can be expected to generate. They calculate fixed and variable costs and eventually either ratify or reject the proposed price. Sales staff is remunerated based on the revenue they generate. It is an open secret at the company that members of its sales staff estimate "win prices" as low as possible to maximize their chances of landing a contract. As a result, there is little mutual trust between Sales and Finance.

Finance managers negotiate the process on autopilot. They do not develop tooling aimed at validating market price estimates consistently, integrally, and factually. This leads to an internal and natural downward pressure on price.

Supply chain
A truck manufacturer moves its European production to a facility in Scandinavia. This facility's financial management uses its own cost allocation method for electric trucks that are in high demand. Consequently, the internal transfer price the production department charges the sales division is higher than the market price the sales division charges its customers. Due to the negative margin, account managers cease their sales efforts for this type of electric vehicle. Based on a technology-led perspective, the head office employs a top-down management approach. It lacks insight into the quality of prices in the supply chain and fails to act on time to define a cost allocation method for production that does justice to variable costs and value in the market.

Supermarkets

With a plethora of prices to deal with, which they also frequently change, supermarkets have a tough job monitoring the quality of their prices. On the reference date of 24 August 2012, Ahold (€10bn in revenue in the Netherlands), for example, uses the same price for a 450-gram jar of own-label strawberry jam as it does for a 600-gram jar of exactly the same strawberry jam, of the same brand (€1.55).[12]

The *per-unit* price will normally be lower for larger packaging or at least be the same. And still, on 20 July 2012, Ahold charges €1.59 for 400 grams of cherry tomatoes in an economy pack, while 250 grams in the regular packaging costs €0.79.[13] The per-unit price is therefore €3.98/kg for 400 grams in an "economy pack". That is 25.8% *more expensive* than the €3.16/kg Ahold charges for regular *smaller* 250 gram trays.

2.3.3 SPEED

The lack of a perspective on pricing has a major impact on the speed with which a price can be set. This speed is particularly important when a price is not a previously set given, such as would be the case with a customized service or product. Speed is also important when a price is no longer adequate, such as when market circumstances have changed or inflation of raw material prices drives up costs.

When a (new) price is not set quickly enough, sales will be affected in terms of volume, revenue, and margin. Customers are sometimes unwilling to accept a delay, and will switch to a competitor who will welcome them with open arms. And if sales staff does still manage to tempt customers to buy, the price may be insufficiently customized. This will erode profitability, as illustrated by the following examples.

International deals

Globally operating suppliers in industries such as IT, mechanical engineering, the automotive industry, staffing, facility, etc. strike cross-border deals with a view to capitalizing on their scale and meeting the needs of major customers. But a global pricing director is often lacking.

An account manager at such a supplier, who wants to quote a price to a customer of the likes of Procter & Gamble, Shell, Vodafone, General Motors, Honeywell, or any other Fortune Global 500 company, will personally have to collect all standard prices from the company's various subsidiaries across the globe. He is the one who gives customers discounts and sets surcharges or margins for customization. He subsequently submits his price proposal to the (central) finance department for approval. A team of financial analysts will then compile a business case. However, this team has little knowledge of the value provided to customers or how accurate sales forecasts are. Nonetheless, the business case they compile passes the desks of all CFOs in the regions and countries concerned for approval. This is a lengthy process that may take up to several months.

One commonly used way of bypassing this sees companies setting up a global unit that enters into and manages global contracts. But the same problem crops up again: forming a good agreement for one hundred countries requires information about costs and market prices from local units. The challenge global deal makers face is to have information about local prices readily available. When the authority for pricing is bestowed on a global unit, central pricing specialists can cut the time spent on drawing up an offer from several months to 24 hours. Pricing managers can, furthermore, tailor the structure of the quoted price to the customer. Deal makers can then rely on support that improves the quality and velocity of sales.

Fashion retail
Retailers of fashion clothing often use one and the same price throughout a season. This retail price was set when the item was launched. Toward the end of the season, any remaining stock will be put into the sale to make way for the next collection. Stores will, however, know well before that which items will remain unsold. Retailers are traditionally slow in using price and discounts as sales tools. They put that off until the sales, missing out on valuable percentages of revenue in the process. Marking down prices of poorly-selling items and raising prices of items that are more in demand will set any retailer on the road toward more revenue. Better pricing will offer retailers who work with narrow net margins much-needed opportunities.

2.3.4 CUSTOMER FOCUS

Customer-driven pricing sometimes puts managers in two minds. They want to make as much as they can from customers, and therefore prefer to limit customer-friendliness to aspects that are not related to price. Financial services providers, for example, prefer not to display customer focus in the transparency of their fees. But customer focus not only plays a major role in transparency, it is also crucial in the pricing model.

In 2010, Dutch mobile telecommunications operators[14] decided to round call charges up to the minute. As a consequence, a 10-second call was charged as a 1-minute call, while a call that took 1 minute and 5 seconds was recorded as a two-minute call. After a wave of protest and pressed by the government, the operators soon reversed the general applicability of the new rounding up rule. They decided, albeit reluctantly, to additionally offer contracts under which calls are charged per second under different rate plans. This coexistence of two charging models has, however, not helped ease market complexity.

Another example: in the late 1990s, Coca-Cola came up with the idea of fitting refrigerated vending machines with a thermometer so as to crank up the price of a Coke as temperatures rise. After all, the hotter it is outside, the more people want an ice-cold Coke. The idea sparked outrage. The *San Francisco Chronicle* branded it "Coca-Cola's cynical ploy to exploit the thirst of faithful customers", while the *Philadelphia Inquirer* concluded that it was "the latest evidence that the world is going to hell in a handbasket". Coca-Cola executive Doug Ivester countered the critique by explaining that paying more under hot weather conditions is fairer, but his retort was to no avail. Coca-Cola soon cut its losses and dropped the idea.[15]

2.3.5 TRAINING

There is little regard for (embedding) pricing skills and development of best practices. In most cases, IT only provides very limited support for pricing. Employees are insufficiently equipped to analyze prices.

Marketing, commercial, and financial education spends little to no time on pricing. General textbooks for courses furthermore tend to exclusively cover largely inferior strategies such as cost-plus pricing and competitive pricing. Subjects that specifically focus on pricing are not part of the compulsory curriculum at business schools and economics faculties.

Employees and managers therefore lack the required knowledge to be able to optimize prices and run and implement processes adequately, even if they have enjoyed an Ivy League education.

2.3.6 QUALITY CONTROL

Companies have control processes in place to monitor the quality of production, the safety of their operations, the correctness of their financial statements, the development of management resources, and the performance of commercial departments, but quality control for pricing is lacking.

Even though the quality of the pricing policy is a major factor in a company's financial health, responsibility for pricing is often placed in the hands of operating companies without expert review of the soundness of pricing decisions. Control is restricted to general financial reports afterwards, which fail to specifically address the pricing policy and the implementation thereof.

2.4 Perspectives in this book

2.4.1 PRINCIPLES FOR PRICING IN THIS BOOK

Part I (The Art of Pricing) will address twelve possible price drivers or principles underlying the selling price (the 12 Cs of pricing). The art of pricing is to select the right revenue model and pricing strategy from these 12 Cs, i.e., those that are best aligned with a company's business model, market, and target customer group.

We will distinguish between price drivers based on performance, transaction, communication, and relationship. This will put the cost price and market price principles into a broader perspective, one that does justice to the vast array of different opportunities that are open to a company.

2.4.2 ANALYSIS AND EXECUTION IN THIS BOOK

Part II (The Science of Pricing) will subsequently go into analysis and research methods that are needed to provide grounding for and eventually implement the pricing strategy. Our approach will be an integrated one, combining commercial managers' knowledge, experience, and intuition with information from readily available data sources. Executive decision makers can then decide in consultation with their pricing managers whether more in-depth and specific research is required to gain more detailed insights.

Part III (The Execution of Pricing) will first discuss the pricing process. We will go into the structure of this process and how it ties in with other primary processes. After that, our focus will shift to the organization of pricing, allocation of responsibilities, access to information, and selection and training of capable human resources. We will conclude with change management aspects of pricing improvements.

The art of pricing

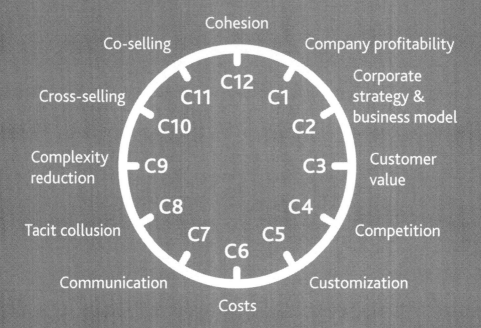

CHAPTER 3

The freedom of pricing

3.1 Pricing as a creative process

People like to pursue clear targets. How well children do at school, for example, is quantified in the form of a grade on a report card. The same linear pattern is used in companies, where commercial management is focused on sales figures, while the CFO pursues clear goals on the level of costs. Targets for success are often one-dimensional.

In the more creative sections of a company, this kind of linear approach is unproductive. Innovations and creative improvements are not the fruit of a pursuit of an unequivocal target, such as a specific number of promising ideas a day. This is the realm of inspiration and perseverance: these are the true sources of innovation.

Numerous managers also take a linear approach to their company's pricing policy. After all, a price is just a number that can only be higher or lower, or so it seems. However, *the* optimum price in an absolute sense does not exist. Pricing is a creative process, regardless of the fact that it involves countless seemingly objective calculations presented by spreadsheet specialists and consultants.

The amount of freedom you have in setting a price is exceptional. There is a huge variety in the different kinds of prices and discounts you can offer, as well as in their level. You can offer certain products free of charge, while charging steep prices for others. You can serve one customer instantly at a high price, while you keep another waiting. You can present a price on a price list solely to influence customers' perception. You can set a price per minute or per ounce, kilobyte, or any other unit. Nobody's stopping you. Other operational decisions tend to be far more dependent on external factors and physical possibilities.

In practice, few entrepreneurs and managers realize that they have such great freedom when it comes to pricing. Whenever you discuss the subject of pricing, they will cite less conscious considerations and implicit rules as decisive for pricing. These kinds of convictions are deeply instilled in the minds of those who count pricing among their duties, obscuring their view of the options available to them. But general principles that were formed in the past are perhaps no longer appropriate for the company or the market. In such cases, untangling the options for improvement turns out to be more complex than initially thought.

Even with a relatively simple measure such as merely raising or lowering a price, things do really get complex when you oversee the consequences of that price change. Lowering a price will, for example, generally boost demand, while cutting the margin. These are two opposite effects on profitability. Your price cut may also prompt your competitors to do the same. That is a third effect. The way you communicate about price subsequently partly determines the impact of price changes, as will a restriction of the validity of the price change, as would be the case with a special offer. All in all, there are a lot of factors to weigh up in setting a price.

The FirstPrice Pricing Clock (FPC) is the point of departure for our explanation of the art of pricing. The FPC contains twelve considerations, or *drivers*, for pricing (see price drivers in Table 1). The FPC unites a number of different directions set out in professional literature, which are rarely linked in publications.

The best pricing managers are those entrepreneurs who are able to create a revenue model that is perfectly aligned with their business model and business philosophy. From the twelve price drivers, they will collate the revenue model that will best enable them to accomplish their business objectives. You are encouraged to do the same.

Focus	Price driver
Performance	(C1) Company profitability
	(C2) Corporate strategy & business model
Transaction	(C3) Customer value
	(C4) Competition
	(C5) Customization
	(C6) Costs
Communication	(C7) Communication to customers
	(C8) Tacit collusion
	(C9) Complexity reduction
Relationship	(C10) Cross-selling
	(C11) Co-selling
	(C12) Cohesion

Table 1 The 12 Cs of pricing and revenue models

3.2 The twelve price drivers

3.2.1 PERFORMANCE

Chapter 4 will go into the objectives and performance of the company. The first price driver is the direct objective of profitability (C1). The second price driver is made up of the objectives of corporate strategy and business model (C2).

3.2.2 TRANSACTION

Chapter 5 will view pricing from the viewpoint of the transaction. We will address the value (C3) that customers assign to an offer within the context of competing (C4) alternatives. This chapter will also focus on the possibility of varying prices from one customer or customer segment to the next (C5). In order to assess the contribution of the above concepts on profits, we will conclude with the cost analysis (C6).

3.2.3 COMMUNICATION

The role of communication is discussed in Chapter 6. With the right communication, you can steer customers and competitors in a subtle way. Customers' perception is influenced by the way in which you inform them on prices (C7). Within certain boundaries, you can exert a positive influence on the market price, as long as you don't see your competitors as enemies (C8). And finally, price engineering will often complicate internal and external communication. In industries such as mobile telephony, energy, or air travel, the average customer will be unable to instantly take in the many thousands of options. Complexity reduction (C9) is then a price driver in its own right.

3.2.4 RELATIONSHIP

Chapter 7 will deal with the return on customer relationships. Putting relationships center stage may clash with transaction-based drivers. How about providing services free of charge as per the "freemium" model? Retailers draw on this same logic when they deploy "loss leaders". These are products with a selling price that is below their cost price, intended to generate footfall, in the hope that these people will also purchase other items.

Cross-selling (C10) requires a relationship with the customer, who will enjoy a direct financial benefit in a transaction. The price you offer is "too low" to further strengthen the relationship with the customer. Co-selling (C11) is based on a value exchange among several parties. This involves giving a discount to one party in order to make more off another party. Co-selling is a tactic often seen at commercial TV stations and Internet companies, but also in large infrastructure projects. Cohesion (C12), finally, is all about mutual relations between price drivers. The chance of success is greater when price drivers work together.

CHAPTER 4

Performance

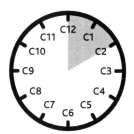

4.1 Objective

What you intend to achieve with the price you decide on will determine the level and structure of your price. In a narrow sense, price is a tool that enables you to boost profitability and your company's value directly. The first price driver is therefore company profitability (C1). This is achieved through the effect price has on sales, revenue, and profits, without considering other factors.

Price can, however, also be a means to ends from the business strategy and business model that reach beyond directly boosting profits. The strategy will in that case determine the pricing objective. When a company, for example, aspires to attain cost leadership, it may choose to lower prices to stimulate sales, banking on economies of scale to lead to lower costs. Corporate strategy and business model (C2) is the second price driver.

This chapter will further detail the two performance-related price drivers.

4.2 Company profitability (C1)

Generating more profit is an obvious price driver, due to the simple fact that price greatly influences sales, revenue, and margin. Entrepreneurs therefore often test prices to see how they affect their bottom line. Direct assessments of the influence of price on profitability do not require in-depth analysis of customers, competition, costs, or other factors. In practice, price testing is mainly performed for small price changes. These involve less risk, meaning that the analysis of the underlying dynamics will not be missed as much.

Annual upward price indexation is a popular way of picking up a little extra profit every year. However, it also forces customers to up their budget every year, which changes the dynamics of the relationship, and may lead to irritation and protest. In 2012, some scientists were so fed up with the increasing cost of scientific journals that they encouraged each other to publish in free open-source journals.[16] The counterargument that what university libraries pay for each article read has dropped over the past years,* as a result of the greater uptake of journals, simply cut no ice with them anymore.[17]

Over the past few decades, companies have enhanced, often instigated by financial controllers, the analysis of their profitability. Where a profit and loss account at overall company level used to suffice, companies now have a lot more information readily available; data warehouses can map profitability for every part of a product and service portfolio. The advantage of this kind of detailed information is that it makes it easier to use price as a tool to achieve the objectives. But there is also a drawback, namely that the information does not provide insight into the underlying reason for profitability, such as the market situation or customer relationships. Also, the cost calculation and profitability analysis are, to a certain degree, subjective (refer to Chapter 2) and generally tailored to finance and tax needs of cost and profit allocation rather than to the objectives of strategic pricing analysis (see also paragraph 5.5).

---

* On a cost basis, the price per download in the U.K. fell for example from £1.19 in 2004 to £0.70 in 2008.

It would therefore be sensible not to put all your eggs in the basket of the first price driver C1, i.e., profitability, in a direct sense. In the following, we will continue with the second price driver, corporate strategy and business model.

4.3 Corporate strategy & business model (C2)

4.3.1 VARIETY OF STRATEGIES AND BUSINESS MODELS

Entrepreneurs' creativity in developing strategies and business models seems to know no bounds. Just look at the number of schools of thought and approaches in the area of business strategy. Strategies and business models set out how to add value. The revenue model and price drivers are a part of that. The strategy will often not define profitability as a direct objective, but rather target more sales, a greater market share, or larger customer base. The second price driver (C2) is the direct objective of the strategy.

The scope of this section will be confined to three important examples of a possible strategy: cost leadership, market dominance, and niche leadership. Maximizing profit in the short term is not the aim. There are other direct objectives, which are intended to lead to greater profits in the long term.

4.3.2 COST LEADERSHIP

When a company seeks to attain "cost leadership" (lowest costs), the short-term goal will be higher sales. Larger volumes will produce economies of scale in the area of production, delivery, and procurement, hence lowering cost per unit. Numerous Chinese manufacturers, but also retailers such as Walmart, Aldi, and Lidl, have adopted this strategy. Aiming for more sales calls for a low price, one that is considerably below the value customers assign to the product. A price that is "too" low will spark demand and "push" smaller providers out of the market.

4.3.3 MARKET DOMINANCE

A second widely-held goal is a dominant market position. Multinationals have been setting targets along the lines of "being number 1 or 2 in every market" for years. They regularly come up with an aggressive pricing policy with an eye to growing their market share. The importance ascribed to market dominance is partly the result of the so-called PIMS studies.[18] These studies into the variables that influence the performance of a large number of companies showed a positive statistic correlation between market share and profitability. Consultants and board members the world over inferred from that outcome that a large market share is what they should be aiming for.

Over the past few years, the importance of market dominance has waned in companies' strategies, and the focus has shifted to alternatives such as niche leadership. This shift was prompted by follow-up studies that cast doubt on the causality of the aforementioned correlation[19] from the original PIMS studies.

4.3.4 NICHE LEADERSHIP

Another possible strategy is to try to conquer a niche. Dominance in a specific section of the market can be based on propositions such as:
- no-frills* (e.g. Aldi)
- value-for-money (e.g. Ikea)
- product leadership (e.g. BMW)
- exclusivity (e.g. Rolex)

These kinds of propositions are exclusively focused on one niche. No-frills suits the lowest market segment, while exclusivity will work best in the highest market segment.

---

* No-frills: keeping cost down by cutting non-essentials in order to be able to charge the lowest possible price.

4.3.5 ALIGNMENT

Whatever the strategic goals may be, a successful pricing policy is always one that has been integrated into the business model. One look at the history of Dutch supermarket chain Albert Heijn shows what happens when pricing policy and business model are misaligned.[20]

Around the turn of the millennium, supermarket holding Ahold used high prices to maximize the returns (C1) of its subsidiary Albert Heijn, the market leader in the Netherlands. Ahold needed resources to fund its acquisition drive, which ended up making this company one of the world's largest retail conglomerates at the time.

It worked out well for them for a while. Supermarket customers are loyal. Most customers shop at the store that is nearest to where they live. And they furthermore always go to the same supermarket for their groceries, because going to a different one would involve having to find their way round a different shop layout and assortment. And yet, after a while, increasing numbers of shoppers started noticing that Albert Heijn's prices were quite high, perhaps even too high for their liking. Customers started turning their backs on Albert Heijn. And it was mainly families that did so: they tend to buy large quantities and could therefore potentially make greater savings on their groceries when shopping elsewhere.

The *high prices* and high *per-item margins* the holding forced Albert Heijn to use went against Albert Heijn's business model, which favors *revenue and absolute per-customer margin* and the *number of customers*. After all, supermarkets and department stores are in the game of making the most of their broad assortment. Attractive prices boost returns by drawing *more customers* (C2) into the shop. Secondly, low prices also tempt customers to buy more products per visit. Earning the highest *absolute per-customer margin (in euros)* (C2) depends more heavily on per-customer revenue than on the relative (percentage) margin per product. The importance of per-customer revenue and number of customers was even greater for Albert Heijn because their assortment is broader than that of its competitors (see Figure

3). All Albert Heijn needed to do was to keenly price items that its competitors also carried.

Albert Heijn would then have been able to "subsidize" these low prices using the margins on items customers could not get at its competitors. That would have been a relatively cheap way of attracting shoppers, and enticing them to buy all their groceries (even the more expensive ones) at Albert Heijn.

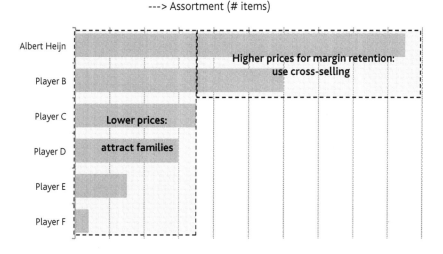

Figure 3 Strategic advantage of Albert Heijn's superior assortment size (fictitious data)

Parent company Ahold failed to factor in the optimum business model when it decided to impose price hikes. This eventually led to a decline in Albert Heijn's market share and profitability. When a boardroom crisis at Ahold liberated Albert Heijn from the yoke of its parent company's rigid pricing ideas, Albert Heijn immediately instated a keener pricing policy. This led to a tremendous rise in the number of customers and revenue, *as a result of which* both profitability and market share grew.

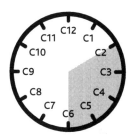

CHAPTER 5

Transaction

5.1 Beyond the flat world

Cost-plus and competitive pricing are one-dimensional and overly simple ways of setting the selling price. These two popular methods lead to a passive attitude. All there is to it is to slap a standard margin on top of the cost price, stay in line with "the" market price, or strike a happy medium between these principles in two dimensions. Some people still seem to believe the world is flat.

For the price drivers that are covered in this chapter the emphasis is on the transaction. A transaction is the exchange of something of value between two parties. Price drivers that are centered on this factor have a broader perspective, as they distinguish more dimensions for pricing. We will look at the factors that determine whether or not transactions come about when customers are free to choose. The central focus will then be on the differences and similarities between options. The differences are determined by the uniqueness of customers, products, or companies. Similarities provide benchmarks against which prices can be offset. The art of pricing is to identify the similarities and appraise the differences.

Customer value (C3) is what a customer thinks your product or service is worth. If that value equals or exceeds the price, a customer will proceed to purchase. Competition (C4) is important in two ways. Firstly because customers use competitors to compare the price-to-value ratio. And secondly, your product's relative value will change as soon as your competitors change their prices. Customization (C5) offers the opportunity of charging certain customers different prices, based on individual value perception. And costs (C6), finally, determine your minimum price. It is important that every price be higher than *avoidable* costs and not higher than the *average total* costs, as is the case with cost-plus pricing.

The four Cs of transaction-driven pricing (C3, C4, C5, and C6) are the core of the domain of pricing that is referred to as value pricing,[*] as taught nowadays at business schools and described in management literature.[21]

5.2   Customer value[†] (C3)

The idea behind value pricing is that customers are willing to pay any price that is below the *value* they assign to a product or service. In pricing, this leads to the principle of customer value (C3), which is also referred to as "willingness to pay". The optimum price mirrors this value. When a price exceeds the customer's perceived worth, there will be no sale, and charging a price that is lower than the willingness to pay is not necessary.

The logic of the value principle is attractive. Innovating, successful, growing companies that charge a value-based price have given value pricing a good name. Apple, Nespresso, and Audi, for example, stood out in a positive sense in 2011 with a combination of value-based prices, satisfied customers, and high profitability. There are,

---

[*] *Customer perceived value pricing* is another widely-used concept. This is an addition that goes with the price driver C7 "communication to customers", which will be covered in Chapter 6.

[†] Customer value: *a customer's assessment of what a product or service is worth.* The term customer value is also used with a wholly different definition, i.e.: *the financial value that serving a customer represents to a company (over the years).* This is not what we are referring to here.

however, three reasons why operationalization of the concepts of value and valuation is far from straightforward.

First of all, customer value is *difficult to observe*, because it is partly a subconscious value and because customers do not always answer honestly when asked about their perception of a proposition's worth. Secondly, this value is not objective, but *subjective*. Perception of a product's or service's worth will differ from one customer to the next. Thirdly, value is *changeable*, because it depends on numerous variables. Value perception will change, for example, due to changes in a customer's budgetary circumstances, economic conditions, shifting preferences, and developments at the competition or in technology.

These are the reasons why it will remain hard to get a grip on value pricing for managers for whom pricing is not their first priority. This will, among other things, lead to resistance during implementation processes, as these need a clear goal and a transparent method for the organization.

Pricing experts are more familiar with these concepts, and use them pragmatically. Their main focus is on the choices customers are making, from which they derive customers' implicit perception of worth. Part II (The Science of Pricing) will go into the operationalization and quantification of concepts such as value and price sensitivity in greater detail. This chapter will cover the conceptual framework and approach.

There are various factors that play a role in the formation of customers' perception of a product's or service's worth. In marketing, these factors are referred to as the "value drivers" or "purchase factors". Purchase factors are the reasons on which a customer bases his or her decision to purchase a product or not. In the context of a simplified example of cars, the value drivers are product-related features and financial factors (see Table 2). The value drivers are not all equally important. In this case, the power of the brand, for example, weighs heavier in the decision to purchase a car than fuel economy (10%).

	Value drivers	Weight
Product-related	Engine	20%
	Model	15%
	Reliability	20%
	Power of the brand	20%
Financial factors	Trade-in value	15%
	Fuel economy	10%

Table 2 Example of value drivers for mid-range cars (fictitious data)

Value is driven not just by the attractiveness of a product. Availability of alternatives also comes into it. Nagle and Holden[22] have split the value of a service or product into two components:

Value = reference value + differentiation value

The alternatives are what determine the "reference value". A customer comparing a €20,000 VW Golf to a €18,000 Kia Cee'd will try to figure out which *unique* features justify the €2,000 price difference. The *reference* value of €18,000 is not questioned as much, as customers perceive that to be "the" market price for that kind of car. The customer's attention goes to the unique premium the VW Golf would have to offer for €2,000.

There are more alternatives than just directly competing propositions. There are four sources of reference value:

Alternatives	Example
Own product/service	VW Golf ⟷ VW Polo
Direct competitor	VW Golf ⟷ Kia Cee'd
Indirect competitor	Car ⟷ motorcycle, train, ...
Delay decision	Keep current car

Table 3 Sources of reference value

Value drivers should be seen in light of the unique value a certain feature can have for customers. Volkswagen is a stronger brand. But a Kia offers a premium in the form of its seven-year warranty, which is longer than the warranty Volkswagen offers. Setting a value-based price therefore requires understanding of customers and value drivers — of the company's proposition and that of the competition.

The price drivers of customer value (C3) and competition (C4) are intertwined. After all, the value of your proposition (C3) partly depends on the alternatives that are available (C4). The price and value of a competing proposition are relevant reference points in defining your price and value. Pricing is then focused on *price-to-value ratios*[*] in the market, and not on market prices.

In closing: for value-based pricing to be applied properly, it needs to be embedded into a value-driven commercial approach. Such an approach should accurately combine three things:
- creation of value in product development,
- communication of value through marketing and sales, and
- generation of revenue from value through pricing.

5.3 Competition (C4)

Together, market price and competition (C4) define the reference value, making them *indirectly* determinative for the value (C3). Value pricing is based on differences (unique value) and similarities (reference value) in relation to competitors or alternatives. This is a more sophisticated approach than competitive pricing, which uses market price as a direct standard. Value pricing uses the price-to-value ratio as the reference point in setting a price.

A "value equivalence" diagram provides insight into market positioning (see Figure 4).[23] With value on the horizontal axis, and price on the vertical, the "equivalence line" denotes the ratio of price to value.

---

[*] These concepts can be further refined to *perceived* value and *perceived* price. Perception can be steered by communication (refer to Chapter 6).

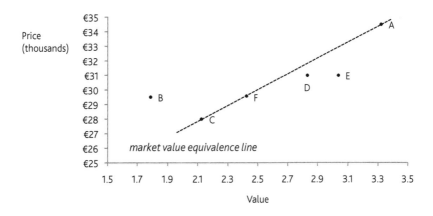

Figure 4 Example of a price-to-value diagram for mid-range cars, whereby 1 = weak, 2 = average, 3 = strong, 4 = excellent (fictitious data)

In a stable market, propositions will be on the value equivalence line, meaning that prices are an adequate reflection of the perceived value. In Figure 4, the prices of A, F, and C are in balance with the market value. E and D, on the other hand, offer a premium, while B is relatively expensive. Table 4 below lists the data on which Figure 4 is based. This table contains prices, value drivers, and their relative weight. (Part II (The Science of Pricing) will go into the methods that can be used to compile this kind of table.)

Value drivers	A	B	C	D	E	F	Weight
Product							
Engine	3	2	2	3	4	3	20%
Model/design	3	2	2	3	2	4	15%
Reliability	3	2	3	3	4	2	20%
Brand	4	2	2	3	3	2	20%
Financial							
Price (thousands €)	34.5	29.5	28.0	31.0	31.0	29.5	N/A
Trade-in value (3y)	75%	60%	62%	65%	68%	62%	15%
Fuel economy	4	1	2	3	2	2	10%
Value estimate	3.3	1.8	2.1	2.8	3.0	2.4	

Table 4 Value drivers for mid-range cars, whereby 1 = weak, 2 = average, 3 = strong, 4 = excellent (fictitious data)

Table 4 tells us that the premium offered by E lies in the value drivers of "engine", "reliability", and "trade-in value". The price for B is relatively high. This car basically scores poorly on all points. The market price principle would, actually, result in a different conclusion about the price of B. The price would then not be considered high, but as relatively low. After all, B is, after C, the cheapest of these cars.

Needless to say, this kind of analysis will be less accurate than a test in a physics lab. But still, useful indications of value that are comparable to weather forecasts or election predictions in terms of accuracy are indeed possible. The methods used will generally point in the right direction and estimate effects within a certain margin of error. Accuracy depends on how the analysis is performed and what budget there is available for data collection.

5.3.1 DEFENDING PRICE AND VALUE

By considering value and price as a unit, you are managing not only pricing effectively, but also your sales department's performance. Good salespeople focus on the value proposition they offer. Whenever a price or value proposition is off target or offers room for improvement, they will give factual and detailed feedback to the pricing manager.

Less-experienced sales staff will, however, not be able to address their losses and successes in terms of value. They will simply brand "the" price "not competitive". These salespeople would benefit from targeted training and an exchange of best practices with fellow top-ranking salespeople, who would then assume the role of change agents.

5.3.2 COMPETING ON PRICE

The price-to-value ratio diagram also provides insight into market *behavior*. Not all price reductions, for example, are an act of aggression. If B from our example were to launch a promotional campaign offering discounts, the price-to-value ratio would lead to us considering that a corrective and defensive move, not an aggressive one.[*] Players A, C, and F will not have to take up their price weapons in defense.

5.3.3 COMPETING ON VALUE

The diagram furthermore shows that improvements that increase value without being accompanied by a price hike are aggressive movements. E is basically already taking up such an aggressive position; E could consider raising its price. Sales would, due to the strong value proposition, probably not see a considerable drop. So all in all, a price rise would likely lead to an increase in the absolute margin.

One example of competing on value can be found in the detergent market. The introduction of an improved formula that delivers better cleaning at lower temperatures is an aggressive move. After all, without an accompanying price rise, the formula would deliver greater value for the same price. A good defense against such an attack is to selectively use the weapon of price through a volume discount (2 for 1) just before the launch date of the competitor's new and improved formula. Consumers will then likely stock up on your detergent, causing slow sales of the new detergent. This will buy you some time to come up with an innovation of your own.

5.3.4 TARGET GROUP

One aspect that the price-to-value diagram sheds insufficient light on is the fact that not all customers or customer groups have the same value perception. A comparison will only hold when manufacturers focus on more or less the same target group. For Mercedes-Benz, for example, the value Chevrolet drivers assign to a Mercedes is less relevant, as Chevrolet drivers are not part of their target group. But they are interested in how customers of other luxury brands perceive their cars. These luxury brands are in their "peer group" or "reference group": manufacturers with the same target group.

---

[*] Again, when going by the market price principle, such a price reduction would be judged differently, and would indeed be considered an aggressive move instead of a defensive one.

The definition of the target group of customers and peer group of competitors is therefore a crucial decision in the implementation of a value-based pricing strategy.[*]

5.4 Customization (C5)

Companies often treat certain customers differently in the sales process. Quality-conscious customers, for example, receive more attention than "bargain hunters". Price customization (C5) allows you to make this same distinction in the pricing policy with a view to making more profit. That would lead to price differentiation: a price customized to a particular sales opportunity.

Price customization is a widely used tactic. What, for example, does a can of Coca-Cola cost? That question is virtually impossible to answer.[24] A better question would be: how many different prices are there for a can of Coca-Cola, and what are they? A can from a vending machine at a sports venue may cost up to €2.50 or more, while that same can in a 24-can pack from the supermarket will only set you back €0.46.

Let's take the example of an orchestra that sells 1,000 tickets to one of its concerts at one uniform price of €35 per ticket, generating revenue of €35,000 (€35 * 1,000) (see the dotted rectangle in Figure 5a). Under pressure from cuts to the orchestra's subsidy, the orchestra's manager decides to start charging two prices. He now offers regular tickets at €50 each. But the venue has a capacity of 1,500 and hardly ever sells out. He therefore decides to charge students and people on a low income €25 per ticket (see Figure 5b). The price rise for the regular tickets is 43%, while the price of the discounted tickets is 29% lower than the previous single price.

---

[*] There may also be differences in value perception within one target group. Someone who drives a company car, for example, will have cost considerations that differ from those of someone who buys his or her own car. Seeing as our focus is on underlying principles, we will not go into such layered details.

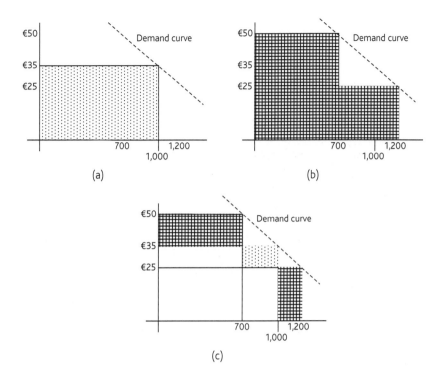

Figure 5 One single price (a) compared to two customized prices (b and c). Price is shown on the y-axis, volume on the x-axis. The surface of the box represents revenue (price x volume).

Thirty percent of those who currently come to the concert are either on a low income or students. A price reduction of €10 enables the manager to sell 500 instead of 300 tickets to this customer segment. The other audience members' decision to come to the concert is not affected by price. They have more money to spend and like going to concerts by the only orchestra in their city. Sales of tickets to these people at the new regular price of €50 therefore remain steady at 700, the same number of people from this segment that bought tickets at €35.

After differentiation in prices, revenue comes in at €47,500. In Figure 5b, this is represented by the checkered surface that results from adding up the amount of €35,000 (€50 * 700) generated by expensive tickets and the amount of €12,500 (€25 * (1,200 − 700)) generated by discounted tickets. We can only conclude that this price differentiation has had a considerable effect. Revenue is up 36% or

€12,500 (€47,500 − €35,000). This rise in revenue is depicted by the surface of the areas of Figure 5b that remain after you subtract the rectangle from Figure 5a. This difference equals the two checkered rectangles minus the rectangle with the black-and-white dots in Figure 5c.

There is also a positive impact on profitability. After all, the costs of staging a concert have remained unchanged except for a slight rise in administrative expenses owing to the fact that the administration now has to handle two types of tickets.

The only downside for the orchestra's manager is that 300 students and people on a low income would also have been willing to pay €35, as we saw prior to the price change. As was to be expected, they gratefully take advantage of the option of buying a ticket to the concert for €25. This special form of price erosion is known as "price dilution". In order to counter price dilution, the orchestra could also start charging two prices for students and people on a low income: €35 for a ticket with the usual terms and conditions and a no-frills "last-minute" ticket for a seat at the back for €25. That would take the number of tickets on offer to three (including the general €50 ticket).

In practice, revenue increases from several percentage points up to 10% are commonplace when using price customization instead of one single price. Given that the costs of implementing differentiated prices are relatively low, the major part of the additional revenue will go straight toward profit. When asked about the impact of differentiation of price and services, former British Airways chairman and CEO Sir Colin Marshall replied:

> "If you can deliver something extra ..., some people will pay a slight premium for it. I want to stress that when I say "slight", I mean precisely that. In our case, we're talking about an average of 5%. On our revenues of £5 billion, however, that 5% translates into an extra £250 million, or $400 million, a year."[25]

The strategy of price differentiation is particularly effective when there are large differences in:

- Customer value (willingness to pay)
  Prices vary based on willingness to pay, such as when one customer segment has greater spending power.
- Variable costs (cost to serve)
  Boosting sales by introducing lower price options is only attractive when variable costs are low, such as when there is overcapacity.

There is a snag though. Although you may be able to achieve a lot through price customization, how do you get one customer to pay €50, while charging others €25? It could lead to indignation among customers, who may decide not to go or try to find ways of being eligible for the €25 ticket. Sales of the regular-priced tickets will subsequently be under pressure and the regular price may erode.

This has triggered several measures aimed at making price customization a success, which are jointly also referred to as "fencing".[26] We will now go into five dimensions where price segmentation can be applied:

- Customer
- Purchasing process
- Product or service
- Volume
- Price conditions and pricing model

5.4.1 CUSTOMER

Willingness to pay differs from one customer to the next. In the case of one-on-one relationships with customers, it is relatively easy to personalize prices. The fee a business services provider charges a law firm will probably be higher than the fee it charges a cleaning company. Consumer markets are less personal, but there is still customization of prices to customers. A food company, for example, can offer a discount when consumers enter a code on their website. Only price-conscious customers will actually go to that trouble.

A situation where customers can choose which price to pay is referred to as "self-selection". Customers will choose for themselves whether or not to go to the food company's website to claim the discount. The costs involved in administering this kind of fencing are low, and customers appreciate the freedom of choice.

5.4.2 PURCHASING PROCESS

A price can be subordinated to the *location* or the *moment* of *booking, sale, payment, or delivery.* When you, for example, book a holiday home early, it will be cheaper. A coffee at the airport is more expensive than a coffee at your local café. Home delivery is more expensive than delivery to a pickup location.

5.4.3 PRODUCT AND SERVICE

Different versions of a product and service are priced differently. Customers whose focus is less on price and more on quality will generally buy more expensive versions. Apple, for example, sold its iPhone 4 at a lower price than the faster iPhone 4S in early 2013, while charging even more for the most advanced model, the iPhone 5. Consumers who have got less to spend will settle for the iPhone 4, while those with the greatest willingness to pay will go for the iPhone 5.

5.4.4 VOLUME

Volume is a popular basis for price customization. The per-unit cost to serve is lower when customers purchase larger volumes. Willingness to pay is also lower, as large customers tend to have more reason to look for low prices. But the ease with which salespeople give volume discounts in practice, such as by using a graduated scale, is not without risk. Large customers' willingness to pay may sometimes be greater, such as when the product or service is important to them or because they have ample budgets. In that case, the discount does not need to be a large one.

There are several focus points that need to be heeded when designing a tiered discount structure. You would, for one, be best off limiting yourself to a small number of discount levels in order to keep complexity low (refer to Chapter 6). Five levels will normally be more than enough. Monetary values form a good basis for setting boundaries for discount levels. "10% discount when you spend €10,000 or more" should be preferred over "10% discount when you buy 1,000 items or more". Monetary amounts are more stable over time, and purchases of multiple products and services are easy to add up.

The boundaries of the tiers should be chosen based on the customer base and competition in the market. Section 2 of Chapter 10 contains an example of this for B2B* software licenses.

For practical reasons, large discounts for large volumes should not be revealed to smaller customers. After all, they will not buy such large volumes. And if they were to see the kind of discounts that are unattainable by them, they may become dissatisfied with the smaller discounts they get for smaller purchases. Discounts should in any case not be too steep, even when it is commercially expedient to offer a low net price. A discount of over 20% reflects badly on the credibility of the gross price list. A better way of offering a very low net price is to only state that net price on the offer or to use a second gross price list (with keener prices) for special cases. A third alternative is to charge fixed surcharges as standard and waive these whenever you want to offer a lower price.

A cumulatively structured tiered discount system will appear more economical to customers (see example in Table 5).

From	Discount
€5,000	5%
€10,000	10%
€25,000	12%
€50,000	13%

Table 5 Cumulative tiered discounts, the listed discount will only be given *from* the threshold amounts

* B2B: business-to-business, these are markets where companies produce goods and services for use by other companies or by public sector parties.

The 10% discount will, in fact, only be given between €10,000 and €25,000. Purchases below €5,000* will not even entitle the customer to any discount at all.

The cumulative tiers may lead you to expect a 10% discount on an invoice of €20,000. But the actual cumulative discount on this invoice amount will only be 6.25% (€1,250):

€0	— on the first €5,000
€250 (5% * €5,000)	— between €5,000 and €10,000
€1,000 (10% * €10,000)	— between €10,000 and €20,000

A graduated scale with cumulative discounts will furthermore mean that the net invoice amount for a somewhat larger order will never fall below the net amount due for a somewhat smaller order. That could happen when discount percentages are applied to the full amount or full volume purchased as discounts abruptly jump to the next level up.

When calculation of discounts is accurately and transparently explained on the price list, both customers and sales staff will soon be familiar with the natural and logical operation of cumulative tiered discounts.

5.4.5 PRICE CONDITIONS AND PRICING MODEL

Price conditions that apply to a purchase and delivery also offer an opportunity for price customization. One example is a 1% prompt payment discount. More complex forms of this kind of discount come about as pricing managers start using different price parameters. For a cell phone, for example, you can take out a monthly contract with a voice allowance and a data allowance. An alternative would be to buy calling and data credit, which you use up as you make calls and browse the Internet ("prepaid"). Price conditions

---

* This works in a way that is similar to that of progressive income tax. Just as you will not be taxed on the amount below the first threshold, customers do not get a discount when they spend under €5,000.

and parameters make a good starting point for price customization to usage patterns.

A pricing model can set the tone for an entire industry. At the start of this century, record companies were having a difficult time as consumers became increasingly unwilling to purchase CDs with full-length albums. The music-buying public wanted more flexibility and turned to illegal downloads of individual tracks. Steve Jobs, however, believed that consumers would indeed be willing to pay for music, if only they could get flexibility. Apple saved the music industry on 28 April 2003 when it introduced *per-track pricing* for music to replace *per-album pricing*. The success of iTunes made selling music online profitable.[27]

The online music service Spotify marked another milestone for the music industry in 2008 when it launched a pricing model that was wholly unrelated to the volume of music consumed. Spotify sells un-limited access to its music database on a subscription basis, charging a fixed monthly fee.

5.4.6 IN CLOSING

Not all attempts to customize prices are successful in the market. It is always conditional on consumers accepting the differentiation. That acceptance was lacking when Coca-Cola introduced a vending machine that automatically raised the price of a can of coke on hot days (refer to Section 2.3.6).

Value pricing uses the price-to-value ratio (C3) as the standard on which to base prices. This worth is defined in relation to alternatives (C4). Price customization (C5) yields extra profits for the salesper-son. It gives customers greater choice and a tailored proposition.

A logical question is subsequently what role costs play in pricing. Indeed, when the price is lower than the costs, the company will run at a loss. The crux of the matter here is how you define costs, which takes us to the next price driver, C6: Costs.

5.5 Costs (C6)

5.5.1 VALUE ADDED

It is not the role of costs (C6) to help define the selling price, as happens in cost-plus pricing. Costs (C6) form a constraint: they are the lower limit for pricing. Viewed from the perspective of the transaction (C3, C4, C5, and C6), a company will not make a profit when the selling price is below the cost price. Above that, there is no upper limit when setting the selling price. Application of the principle that income should exceed expenditure requires a correct and integrated cost calculation. This calculation differs from what accountants, bookkeepers, and financial managers are used to, because it has a different purpose.

A cost evaluation as needed by a pricing manager is focused on value added instead of the "right" allocation of costs across products, departments and business units from the perspective of "fair" performance measurement or tax considerations. It will not offset the *specific* price against *average* cost, but expressly consider variable costs. The principle is twofold:
1. the price per *specific* transaction is greater than the *specific* costs of such a transaction
2. the *average* price is greater than the *average* costs

Another difference in comparison to traditional calculations is that we are not using retrospective costs from the profit and loss account[*]. The pricing manager's approach revolves around the combination of:
- *avoidable*, *variable* costs
- *alternative* costs or *dilution*
- a *relevant forecast* of future costs

In the remainder of this section, these three perspectives will be reviewed one by one. At the end of the section we will look at costs and price as part of a holistic management approach.

---

[*] On an organizational level, this different approach leads to a need for clear and comprehensive alignment of the method with financial management.

5.5.2 AVOIDABLE, VARIABLE

Throughout the 1970s, American Airlines[28] only filled half the seats on its planes. It mainly targeted business travelers. When the U.S. government relaxed market regulations, charter airlines suddenly found they could offer flights on a broader scale. These market entrants had fewer overheads and they had great success selling cheap tickets to non-business passengers. Purchasing factors such as punctuality and flexibility are not as important to this customer segment.

American Airlines was the first major airline to act on the knowledge that the *avoidable* costs of empty seats are very minor. These avoidable costs are the *variable* costs of fuel, service, and sales efforts for only one extra passenger at a time. Revenue generated through business passengers "covers" the non-avoidable, fixed, costs of airplane, crew, and overheads.

> "If we could figure out a way to sell those empty seats at the prices the charter guys proposed, thought [American's CEO Robert] Crandall, we would make a lot of dough."[29]

American introduced super saver fares for tourist travel and family visits. The company succeeded in selling a significant number of the available seats that used to stay empty. The percentage of occupied seats, the occupancy rate, went up by a hefty 50%.

5.5.3 ALTERNATIVE COSTS

Loss of income from business travelers is a risk you run when you start selling cheap tickets to tourists. When your business customers also decide to start buying super saver tickets, they will effectively be paying a price that is lower than the price they are willing to pay. These are the *alternative* costs, which is also referred to as dilution.

American, however, managed to implement effective fencing methods for its fares (C5). The company saves customers who pay higher fares a seat on their planes. Inventory management systems predict demand for tickets for every flight and limit availability of cheap fares whenever necessary to make sure premium customers can always get a seat. Restrictive conditions for super saver fares, such as advanced booking, no cancellation, and a minimum stay, mean that lucrative business customers will prefer to pay a premium for tickets without restrictions. Additional benefits for loyal customers, such as frequent flyer miles and lounges at airports, have further bolstered customer loyalty.

The method American Airlines uses is referred to as revenue management. Revenue management draws on the understanding of avoidable, alternative, and future-oriented costs, when these are dynamic and dependent on scarce and temporarily available capacity. Apart from in the airline industry, this discipline is currently also increasingly deployed in industries such as shipping, road haulage, hotels, stadiums, car rental, holiday homes, fashion stores, production capacity, etc.

5.5.4 RELEVANT AND FUTURE-ORIENTED

Pricing decisions have an effect in the future, not in the past; future costs are therefore important for pricing. The average price when launching a new product may initially be below cost price. As sales grow, economies of scale will subsequently reduce costs. Price driver C6 takes the expected future cost price as its reference point.

Cost analyses are often based on past performance, simply because that is data that can be found in the accounts. Finance then uses these past costs in combination with the high-level input from senior management to make a budget for the future. Pricing managers, however, need far more profound insight into product development and R&D to be able to estimate the economies of scale and the flexibility that may or may not exist in cost commitments inherent in for example labor agreements, real estate rental contracts or in the financial setup of production facilities than they can obtain from the limited detail of traditional budgets.

5.5.5 QUANTUM BUSINESS

Business is often presented as a linear process. A new product or service is born out of a flash of inspiration, an idea, regardless of whether it is a brilliant one. The inventor or R&D department will take that idea and turn it into an invention, apply for patents, and mount a production process (first business skill).

Next, the entrepreneur faces the challenge of selling the newly developed product (second business skill). No matter how fantastic the new product is, potential customers simply do not know it yet. Marketing and sales departments will therefore spring into action to spread the happy news, preferably on a grand scale and involving a little pushing, seduction, and manipulation, all for a good cause. Based on our belief, or pretend belief, in our product, we expect part of the market to eventually appreciate the improvements we are bringing, prodded by some gentle pressure from advertising and PR.

This is the basis for a "realistic conservative" forecast of sales and expected average cost price. The selling price is obtained by adding a profit mark-up and possibly adapting the price to "the" market price.

These steps follow each other in a linear fashion. Each step determines the next one in a cause-and-effect relation (see Figure 6). This process can have one of two outcomes: success or failure. Success means the product is profitable and customers are happy, while failure will lead to a cessation of production.

Some entrepreneurs do things differently. They start with the end in mind. When you estimate beforehand what a customer will be willing to pay, you can optimize the cost structure as you develop a product, and vice versa. The entrepreneur will then optimize price and cost simultaneously as a "quantum business" (we are introducing this term by analogy with quantum mechanics, which changed the perspective of cause and effect in physics from a sequential to a simultaneous link).

Figure 6 Business as a linear process

Connection (c) in Figure 7 depicts the mutual alignment of price and costs. This is important in manufacturing the product, setting up the production process, and defining price customization and volume discounts. In sourcing, you will select suppliers that can anticipate and adapt to your needs.

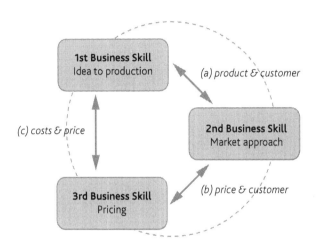

Figure 7 Business as a simultaneous process

Steve Jobs simultaneously optimized product, design and cost, sales opportunities, and price.[30] Apple's functional and top-down organization continuously weighs up costs of raw materials, design of components, and value of product and design against each other. The superior quality of the glass in iPhone and iPad touch screens was one of the results. During the design stage of these devices, Apple factored in procurement costs and economies of scale of its supplier, as well as the value and price of the end product.

5.5.6 IN CLOSING

In Chapter 4 we dealt with the performance-based price drivers (C1, C2). This chapter revolved around the aspects of an optimum price in a transaction. We discussed the importance of the relative value (C3) you provide in comparison to competitors or alternatives (C4). And we also saw that it pays to customize prices to different "price segments" whenever there are differences in willingness to pay or cost to serve (C5). And finally, costs (C6) are the lower limit for a selling price from the perspective of the transaction. With every transaction, the specific price needs to be higher than the avoidable costs. The *average* price of total sales must be higher than the total *average* costs.

As pointed out earlier, the FirstPrice Pricing Clock makes two additions to the six price drivers we have covered so far. The first is the use of communication in improving prices. The second addition is boosting returns on relationships with customers, stakeholders and/or users through pricing.

Chapter 6 will go into price drivers that involve communication (C7, C8, and C9). Chapter 7 will subsequently focus on the relationship-oriented price drivers (C10, C11, and C12).

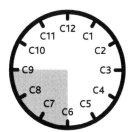

CHAPTER 6

Communication

6.1 Perception drives behavior

A fundamental ongoing debate among economists deals with the nature of economic behavior. This debate pitches two perspectives against each other.

The neoclassical school of thought considers people's economic behavior an essentially rational phenomenon. The ratio of price to volume of demand allows logical understanding and objective determination. Demand for a product is connected to the price and worth of that product in a market owing to its knowable purpose. This notion is comparable to classical mechanics' description of the earth's orbit, which says that the earth's orbit is dependent on the weight and movement of other celestial bodies. The transactional price drivers which we discussed in the previous chapter can be considered to adhere to the neoclassical school of thought.

The other approach is of a more humanist and social nature. This is an approach rooted in psychology, a perspective that does not assume economic behavior to be rational. People's motives are, after all, subjective, as well as often subconscious and inconsistent. Perception and beliefs are what drives behavior, and the way in which you communicate therefore influences the choices consumers and companies make. This chapter is based on this way of thinking.

What we will be exploring is customers' perception when they evaluate prices. The way in which price is communicated will determine people's impression of their options. This is the next price driver (C7). In the following we will look at patterns of implicit communication between competitors that influence price levels in a market to a certain degree. This is what we refer to as tacit collusion (C8). The last communication-related price driver delves into information processing in relation to prices. Companies can refine prices to such an extent that price management almost becomes impossible. Complexity reduction (C9) will then be required to manage communication and alignment in the supply chain.

6.2   Communication to customers (C7)

This price driver shows that communication of prices has an effect on customers' choices. Experimental behavioral science describes a number of effects that marketing and pricing managers target in their communication and pricing. We will go into the relativity of prices and the effect of price "anchors", which provide customers with a point of reference. Following on from that, we will discuss communication about uncertainty and the good-better-best pricing tactic. We will subsequently conclude with the "fairness" of price changes and the intended purpose of "psychological prices".

6.2.1   RELATIVITY OF PRICES

It may not be something you dwell on every day, but money is an abstract variable that renders an air of quantifiability to perceptions of wealth and possession. We use monetary values such as our salary, prices, or our bank balance for all kinds of calculations. That works rather well: when you earn €2,000 a month, after tax, and your rent is €750, you will have €1,250 left for other expenses.

But perceptions of wealth and possessions are hard to quantify objectively. The scale on which we *perceive* money can therefore not be accurately captured in a numerical value. If an income of €2,000 makes us feel reasonably happy, €4,000 will not automatically make us twice as happy. In 1959, Japanese researcher Tarow Indow concluded from an experiment with his students that in order to acquire a watch they considered twice as desirable as another watch, they were willing to pay 8.7 times as much. Harvard psychologist Stevens ran an experiment that led him to conclude that his students were twice as happy when they unexpectedly received four times as much money.[31]

The relativity of prices also comes to the fore in the way people respond to a windfall.[32] In 1985, Richard Thaler described how his respondents preferred winning $25 and $50 in two lotteries to winning $75 in one lottery. Thaler's advice was therefore "not to wrap up all Christmas presents together in one box". By accurately and separately highlighting all aspects of a product in marketing and advertising material, a consumer's perceived value of that product will increase.

The "Permanent Discount" rail card offered by Dutch rail operator NS is a fine example of that, and certainly lives up to its name. NS lists the various benefits of this rail card on its website (see Figure 8).[33]

Permanent Discount rail card
Do you regularly take the train to work, school, or just to go on a day out? The Permanent Discount rail card will give you a discount whenever you travel! Both during the week and on weekends.

- Always a discount, no matter when you travel
- 20% discount during peak hours
- 40% off-peak and weekend discount
- 40% discount for co-travelers after 9am and on weekends the whole day (max. 3 persons)
- Are you over sixty? For only €14 (2nd class) or €39 (1st class), you get 7 additional days of your choice on which you travel for free
- Annual rail card €20 per month, i.e., €240 per annum
- Monthly rail card €25 per month

Figure 8 Example of "discount on top of discount" to appear even more economical

6.2.2 ANCHORS

The attractiveness of a price is generally not tangible or quantifiable to people as a real number, but prices are *comparable*. It is easier to assess which price is *higher* than another than to assess *how* high one price is. People subconsciously look for help in their environment in these situations, and are susceptible to insinuation. They look for an "anchor" on which to base their assessment. When judging a price, the anchor, quite remarkably, does not have to have any rational link to that price.

One experiment[34] asked participants to enter the last two digits of their social security number on a form. Having done so, they were subsequently asked to bid for two bottles of wine, a 1998 Côtes du Rhône and a 1996 Hermitage. The researcher told the participants that the Côtes du Rhône came with a quality rating of 86 points, while the other wine had a rating of 92 points.

It turned out that the higher the last two numbers of someone's social security number, the higher their bid! Subconsciously, the social se-curity number apparently offered a (totally irrational) anchor. The participants did, however, bid more for the Hermitage than they did for the Côtes du Rhône. This is in line with the ratings. Contrary to how much they bid, the outcome of the price *comparison* between the two products was rational.[*] Assessing the level of a price can be arbitrary, but price comparisons are generally more consistent.

Nobel Prize winner Daniel Kahneman and his colleague Amos Tversky are among the architects of "behavioral economics". This discipline within the field of economics studies people's behavior using empiri-cal research and experiments. In 1974, Kahneman and Tversky dem-onstrated the "anchoring"[35] effect in their famous "United Nations" experiment. In this experiment, a participant would first observe a wheel of fortune that was made to stop either on 65 or 10 (the wheel was manipulated to only point at either 65 or 10 to simplify the ex-

---

[*] It is unclear how *objective* the ratings of the wine were. Participants were only told that the rating came from different specialist wine magazines.

periment). Having seen the wheel point to either 65 or 10, the participant would subsequently be asked to estimate what percentage of countries in the United Nations are in Africa.

Participants' estimates turned out to be related to the number the wheel of fortune had shown them. Those participants who had observed the wheel stop at 65 estimated that around 45 percent of UN countries are African. If the wheel had pointed to 10, this estimate was around 25 percent. What is striking here is that the participants *knew* that the outcome of the wheel was random, and that it was in no way related to the question they were asked.

Needless to say, this experiment set the academic community thinking. Multiple follow-up experiments were organized.[36] These all confirmed the effects of anchors. It emerged that the anchoring effect does not disappear when participants are given a financial incentive to be more accurate in their estimate, and neither when anchors have extreme values. Absurdly high anchors, such as a $7,000 book, have the same influence as "more plausible" anchors. Anchors have also been shown to affect professional experts, such as realtors, despite the fact that they so confidently claim that they cannot be influenced.

In the luxury segment, shops like to show a limited number of highly exclusive and extremely priced items. These products are not directly intended to be sold, but only serve as an anchor. Thanks to these anchors, "regular" big-ticket items will suddenly seem more attainable and sell better.

Coach, for example, a retailer specializing in luxury handbags and accessories, likes to display one or two ultra-expensive handbags in full view and with the price tag clearly showing at its flagships stores. Its range contains for example a $7,000 crocodile leather handbag and an almost identical ostrich leather bag that costs $2,000. By making sure shoppers see the $7,000 price tag for the former bag, the $2,000 price tag for the latter will suddenly not seem so steep.[37]

Anchoring also works in negotiations. Although negotiations may take longer when you start high, research has shown that starting high leads to better end results.[38] And the first blow is half the battle: being the first to name a price means that you are dropping anchor, and it is near to impossible for the other party to ignore that anchor. In negotiations, price is not so much an expression of what someone wants or needs, but rather of what someone thinks they can get. Negotiation training at business schools always teaches executives to use the anchoring effect and to be prepared for when the other party uses this technique. Convincing executives of the fact they too are susceptible to these subconscious processes is no easy task.[39]

It is in any case expedient to study people's choices in a realistic setting. A company can derive great benefits from experiments with pricing and different forms of sales and communication. It is always a good idea to test what works best for your products and your customers.*

6.2.3 UNCERTAINTY

Uncertainty plays a role in the introduction of new products and services and when entering into long-term contracts. The value of contracts can, after all, change over time due to inflation and currency risk. People tend to choose certainty over uncertainty, but there are nuances to this statement. It has, for example, been demonstrated that most people choose avoiding a loss over the chance of earning a profit. This phenomenon is referred to as "loss aversion". A second nuance concerns communication. The way in which you describe the uncertainty will influence customers' choices. We will explain this using a price indexation example.

Inflation leads to uncertainty about future prices. Most people therefore go for contracts with inflation indexation. The influence of communication becomes clear when we compare the following descriptions:

---

* Also refer to Part II (The Science of Pricing).

A. the "certainty" of contract prices with inflation indexation *in real terms*

B. the "uncertainty" of contract prices with inflation indexation *at a level you do not know yet*

Options A and B both offer inflation indexation and basically say the same thing. And yet, A is preferred by relatively more people. Option B wrong-foots some people.[40] Customers are partly led by alarming wording in contracts. They assess risks differently due to the way they are communicated.

6.2.4 GOOD-BETTER-BEST PRICING

The good-better-best (GBB) strategy consists of offering a product or service in three versions:
- good: the basic version
- better: a better version
- best: the top-of-the-range model

Price is in step with quality here: best is the most expensive, good the cheapest, and better, you guessed it, lies somewhere in between.

A salesperson can use this strategy to do three things:
- uncertainty reduction by offering the better version
- anchoring effect of the high reference price of the best version
- competition on low prices using the good version

Marketing professionals often glorify these three versions with appealing names such as silver, gold, and platinum service conditions. The fact that even the cheapest version has a swish name also helps. Silver conditions are better than bronze ones, so just imagine how great the gold and platinum conditions are!

Other manifestations of this phenomenon include L/XL/XXL designations for drinks and food, expert/professional/ultimate for sports gear, or for example take up!/move up!/ high up! for the Volkswagen up!.

Uncertainty reduction will ensure most people go for the better version, simply because that is the safest bet. The price of the better version therefore has the greatest impact on financial results. A high price for the best version will lead to a favorable *anchoring* effect for the price of the middle version. The price of the better version will be made to look more attractive, and can be raised slightly, which would not be possible if the anchor of the higher price for the best version were to be absent.

The price of the good version is a rewarding marketing tool that is used to improve the price image or attract shoppers to your store, website, or brand. The good version is less important from a revenue point of view, as people's uncertainty reduction tendency will drive them not to choose the lowest-quality product at the actual moment of purchasing.

Figure 9 Example of good, better, and best price points

Sales of better or best versions can be further stimulated, at the expense of the good version, by varying the placement of products from these segments in the store or on the website. Anthropological research has shown that people are less likely to buy products that are placed low down on the shelves because that requires them to bend down. Products placed at upper body height sell best: they are easy to grab and the most visible. Studies have also shown that products sell better when they are in the right-hand part of consumers' field of vision.[41]

6.2.5 FAIRNESS AND PRICE CHANGES

Consumers want "fair" prices. But what exactly that means is unclear. As pointed out earlier, consumers do not really have an opinion about the absolute level of a price. So when a price rises, what they tend to look at is the *change*, not the *absolute level* of the price. A clear explanation and understandable selection of arguments are what makes the difference. Arguments based on "cost pressure" or "inflation" are more likely to be accepted than those based on "scarcity in supply".

Naturally, some gumption also comes into it. Manufacturers will often introduce new packaging containing less of a product, but without changing the price. Sales to loyal users will go up by 10%, because they run out of the product sooner. Customers are less likely to notice these kinds of hidden price rises.

Another way of reducing transparency is to make it more complicated to calculate the per-item price. The options Pampers offers its customers in terms of diapers and pack sizes make it harder to compare prices. Take Pampers' options for size 5 diapers, for example:[42]

- 45 diapers "Baby Dry value pack junior" at €15.25
- 38 diapers "Simply Dry Junior" at €10.16
- 26 diapers "Easy up small pack junior" at €10.99
- 62 diapers "Baby Dry jumbo pack junior" at €19.49
- 38 diapers "Active fit value pack junior" at €15.25
- 54 diapers "Active fit jumbo pack junior" at €19.99

Both the number of diapers per pack and the price are never "round". Extrapolating a per-diaper price requires just a little too much effort, making it more difficult to compare prices. Customers will subsequently base their choice on other aspects.

Seeing as price rises resonate negatively, while price reductions come across as positive, Dutch supermarket chain Albert Heijn uses an interesting system that was laid bare by two students, Thijs van der Tuin and Matthijs Neppelenbroek.[43] One day, they decided to keep track of all of Albert Heijn's price changes. Eighteen months later, they had counted more price cuts (15,000) than price rises (5,500), while across the board prices were higher. That was down to the fact that the average price rise was 35 cents, while the average price cut was 12 cents. Apparently, Albert Heijn thought it better to have its customers take the "pain" of a price rise in one go, and give them the "pleasure" of a price cut in small doses. What is more, Albert Heijn does not broadcast price rises, while even small price cuts are widely publicized in their supermarkets and adverts.

In response to the discovery by the two students, Albert Heijn said that "the analysis failed to factor in changes in size" and that "prices are dynamic". "We never said we would not raise prices ever."[44] It is clearly not easy for a company to defend its morality when its tricks have been revealed. The changes in size Albert Heijn invokes work both ways. And it also remains to be seen how credible customers find announcements of price cuts when prices rise so much more than they are reduced.

6.2.6 PSYCHOLOGICAL PRICES

Psychological prices are prices that end in 9, 95, 98, or 99. The reason behind using these prices is that a price of 9.99 *feels* cheaper than a price of 10 euros. A price of 9.99 is thought to generate more sales than a price of 10 euros for the same product. As the salesperson realizes more sales, the "investment" of 1 cent per item will hardly be noticed.

Scientific research into the effects of psychological prices has, however, so far not been able to corroborate that such pricing tactics actually work.[45] Due to the fact that it is such a widely used tactic, customers may infer different messages from these price endings. Some customers turn out to expect a good deal when seeing a psychological price. Others see it as a ploy and subsequently mistrust the shop's general pricing. It is therefore important that these psychological prices tie in with brand perception and positioning. Tests can show which of the two abovementioned effects of psychological prices is the dominant effect among your customers.

6.2.7 IN CLOSING

In this section, we looked at the relevant effects of communication in relation to pricing. Behavioral psychology teaches us that people's buying behavior is often marked by irrational patterns. These subconscious choices consumers make cannot be predicted with any great certainty based on previous scientific studies. That makes it wise to test out within your own sales environment which prices, sales techniques, and combinations of products return the best results.

So far, we have based ourselves on competitors that are vying with us in courting the favors of customers, with price playing an important role. In our discussion of transaction-based drivers, we highlighted the importance of the value of the proposition. Price is an expression of added value in comparison to competitors. You can improve your competitiveness by customizing your prices and hence tap new customer segments. This section focused on the price communication that can also convince customers to buy your product.

The next section will go into ways in which the role of price can be *reduced* and the hatchet of competition can all but be buried.

 ## 6.3 Tacit collusion (C8)

6.3.1 THERE ARE ONLY LOSERS IN WAR

Sales departments in certain industries are often marked by an aggressive atmosphere. Projects are run from war rooms. The mere mention of a competitor's name will make many a manager grimace. Although this animosity may forge a winning spirit in a team, it is not conducive to sensible pricing. Pricing requires a more prudent consideration of positions, competitors, and their behavior. Pricing-savvy companies, therefore, are less macho and more measured in their actions. They take a broader view, surveying all opportunities the market as a whole offers for all providers.

Competition on quality and within specific target groups is more worthwhile than aggressive direct competition on price. The price driver of tacit collusion (C8) helps keep prices in a market at a sustainably healthy level.

6.3.2 COMMUNICATION TO COMPETITORS

Tacit collusion relies on a kind of communication about prices that differs from that of the price driver from the previous section. Communication for tacit collusion is communication to the market instead of to customers.

Collusion is collaboration between two or more parties aimed at dampening competition. There are two forms of collusion: *overt* collusion and *tacit* collusion. Overt collusion is a conscious and explicit deal between competitors, as in a cartel. To protect consumers, this form of collusion is banned in free markets. In 1929 however, Chamberlin[46] identified the phenomenon of *tacit* collusion, which sees companies look for a price level that maximizes revenue for all providers. These providers have all become aware of the fact that competition on price will not win them greater market share. After all, competitors always neutralize a price cut by following suit.

Tacit collusion emerges in transparent markets with a small number of competitors and little differentiation on product level. Two or three providers tend to dominate in a local market, such as in the mobile telephony market, gas stations, in infrastructure, and in flight routes. When the threshold for entry or exit is high,[*] these parties know that they will have to generate revenue together for a long time. Their behavior then becomes less aggressive, as market players match each other's price rises.

The term tacit collusion suggests patterns in market behavior, whereby providers decide, for their own best interest, not to compete on price. However, they do not enter into agreements with competitors about this, neither in writing, nor verbally, nor in any other way. This behavior is the result of repeated experiences in the market that always lead to the same conclusions and outcome. Market players hence develop fixed responses.

---

[*] This is the case when start-up investments are high. Start-up investments include capital items, landing rights, locations, and licenses.

Price driver C8 requires that we factor in these tacit patterns. Our actions generally adhere to unwritten rules, which we will only break after having carefully weighed up the consequences.

6.3.3 COMPETITION REGULATIONS: AN EXAMPLE

This kind of market behavior is a tricky phenomenon for competition authorities. The situation on the Dutch gasoline market proves that.[47] Dating back to the 1990s, Dutch authorities have been investigating unlawful market behavior, possibly based on illegal agreements. They acted on the suspicion that gas prices in the Netherlands were kept artificially high. In the five-year period between 1996 and 2001, for example, the bare price of a gallon of gasoline (i.e., exclusive of sales tax and fuel duty) in the Netherlands was 10% higher than in Belgium, 19% higher than in Germany, and 17% above the European average.

Oil companies suggested that the costs involved in loyalty schemes for consumers, high density of gas stations, and strict Dutch environmental requirements caused this difference.[48] These same oil companies, however, give financial support to local gas station proprietors who are faced with competition on price. These proprietors are paid an amount (margin contribution) that compensates the lower local price level. This enables these proprietors to discourage a local price war by charging even lower prices. In game theory, this is what is called a credible threat, urging all providers in the area to compete on any factor but price.

A 2002 study by the Netherlands Competition Authority (NMA)* concluded that this kind of support to gas station proprietors was objectionable, as it was thought to engender "supracompetitive" prices.[49] But they never found any proof of *price-fixing* agreements in the gasoline market. In 2011, Maxime Verhagen, the then minister of economic affairs, reported to parliament that the gasoline market was "functioning properly".[50]

---

* The Dutch equivalent of the U.S. Department of Justice's Antitrust Division

Tacit collusion is legal, as long as there are no agreements between market parties and no one holds considerable *market power*. In case of doubt, the best thing to do to be on the safe side is call in legal experts to assess the situation and always abide by legislation.

6.3.4 PRICE LEADERS AND PRICE SIGNALS

A market where tacit collusion has appeared is often one with a "price leader". This is the party who is the first to change its price in response to external factors. The price leader is often also the market leader. Van Damme provided an example in 2002, when he noted about the Dutch gasoline market that "Shell's recommended retail prices are also followed by resellers of competing brands".[51] The other parties in the market are called "price followers". Price followers charge the same price as the price leader, or maintain a fixed "price distance". All patterns in pricing behavior are implicit. There are no agreements.

The status quo in a market where tacit collusion reigns is delicate. There is always a lurking danger of something unsettling this status quo. Clarity from all players will help sustain the equilibrium. This requires consistent and clear communication. Market players use "price signals" on two levels for that:
1. Pricing
2. PR policy

Pricing
A company can use its prices to express its opinion on its competitors' prices. Response patterns will soon produce results in markets with electronic price distribution systems and with players with a dedicated price management structure.

In the airline industry, one airline will generally be the dominant party and price leader at its hub.[52] This airline decides what a healthy price level is for a certain route from that hub. If a challenger to this dominant position were to emerge, the price leader can use price changes on other routes to put the challenger in its place. The dominant airline will do so by temporarily charging extremely low prices, preferably in market segments in which the airline it is looking to correct has concentrated most of its operations.

A fictitious example is that of a U.S. airline based in Chicago that wants to attract more transatlantic business. The company starts offering a low fare of 349 euros for flights to the U.S. on the German market. Chances are that the market leader for flights between Germany and the U.S. is not happy with this form of underselling by the Americans. In reply, this dominant party in the German market could decide to introduce an extremely low fare of 99 dollars for flights from Chicago to Germany. This would hit its U.S. competitor directly at its hub. And only offering this extreme fare of 99 dollars for flights to Germany is a clear hint as to the reason behind this price signal.

Seeing as all prices immediately show up in electronic distribution systems, the pricing manager of the US-based airline will probably quickly discontinue the promotion in Germany. Its German competitor might then respond by also revoking its cheap fare. Owing to the speed of the systems involved, these kinds of tit-for-tat signaling techniques can unfold within a time span of only a few hours.

PR policy
A second price signaling method is provided by the PR policy. This policy will be effective when all public announcements about price developments issued by a company are consistent and clear. Reasons behind price changes must be predictable and credible. Commonly used reasons include inflation, higher costs of raw materials, or general worries about the health of the industry. Even if the argumentation is factually correct, a price leader often takes the opportunity to raise prices by more than strictly necessary. It is hard for authorities to identify unlawful acts if there aren't any that violate the *letter* of the law, because companies communicate in a well-considered manner and only through public channels.

Here's an example: container shipping company Evergreen gradually raised its rates from 1 January 2012. Market leader Maersk responded with a nearly 100% price hike. Many other shipping companies followed suit. The Dutch association of shippers, EVA, was startled by this illogical price development in a time of surplus capacity. It called on the European Union to keep a watchful eye on this situation.[53] But the companies involved were only raising prices and making public statements about cost developments, and not breaching any competition legislation.

6.3.5 PROFITABLE PRICE WARS

The principle underlying tacit collusion is a desire to maintain equilibrium and avoid competition on price. A price war can, however, in some cases also turn out to be profitable, if it brings sufficient:
- growth of the market
- growth in market share
- cost savings

Cost leadership through economies of scale and great market potential are in this case important prerequisites. The Chinese market has seen successful price wars that were started by, for example, Changhong (TVs) and Galanz (microwave ovens), but also among Chinese manufacturers, price wars often do not yield the desired result.[54]

6.4   Complexity reduction (C9)

Pricing specialists consider a specific price for each customer the ultimate goal of price customization (C5). Communication subsequently requires even more price points, which are to trigger the anchoring effect during the purchasing process (C7). A company that has enthusiastically taken to deploying price drivers will therefore see the scope and complexity of its pricing structures increase. One way of staying on top of those pricing structures is to hire more pricing analysts and use more specialist IT systems to manage prices. The danger is that the board, sales managers, and service staff lose their handle on the complexity of prices. A lack of pricing transparency leads to suboptimal decisions at the company. Customers too are left with a negative impression of the company. How many customers are positive about air fares, cell phone charges, or photocopier service charges? Complex prices put customers off from buying your goods.

Complexity reduction (C9) is an often neglected price driver at companies that are taking their first steps toward a better pricing policy. And yet it is important to, right from the start, keep structures simple and explain them clearly. A less complex price list can, nonetheless, still be very comprehensive. The idea is to ensure that pricing policy is easy to explain and transparent, not only to customers, but also to colleagues at your company.

Google, for example, has a specific advertisement rate for each keyword. This price is determined through an auctioning mechanism. It therefore has a huge collection of prices for all possible keywords. And still, prices for a Google ad are not complex. Customers will only see the rate for the keyword they are interested in. Internally, the logic behind that is easy to explain. Each keyword is sold to the highest bidder, i.e., the person for whom the keyword represents the greatest worth.

Another example: laptop price customization. This is based on product customization. Again, simplicity is better than a profusion of prices and products. Who else but Apple can accomplish complexity reduction and simplicity? Let's compare the product offering of Apple and Dell on 20 February 2012.

Dell has three different laptop lines (Inspiron, XPS, and Alienware) and offers a plethora of options on top of that, such as five different screen sizes and six possible processors (i3, i5, i7, Atom, Pentium dual core, and Celeron dual core).[55] You can "land" on various different webpages when shopping for a laptop on Dell's website. There is a page with a few good deals only, but also one with the most popular products, and a page with a comprehensive "overview" of all possibilities. And that while Dell has simplified its website in recent years.

In its online store, Apple dedicates only one page to laptops. The choices are simpler: two laptop lines (MacBook Air and Pro), four screen sizes, and two types of processor (i5 and i7).[56] Design and information are instantly clear, because complexity is low at Apple and subordinate to the objective of helping customers.

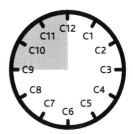

CHAPTER 7

Relationship

7.1 You have to spend money to make money

This chapter is about revenue models that focus on utilizing relationships. Low prices, for example, can provide a way of striking up or strengthening relationships.

Cross-selling (C10) revolves around the one-on-one relationship between salesperson and customer. The salesperson entices the customer to purchase by offering a discount and then makes a profit on subsequent transactions with this customer. A building contractor, for example, may submit a low tender for a road building contract put out to tender by the local council. Profits will subsequently be made on related follow-up contracts that are awarded to the contractor privately.

Co-selling (C11) is aimed at capitalizing on the value that customers or users may represent. Facebook sells the attention of its users ("co"-selling) to advertisers. In essence, Facebook is not a free service, as users pay for this social network with their attention.

Cohesion (C12), finally, describes mutual relations between price drivers. They are, after all, not stand-alone entities: price drivers in a revenue model should reinforce each other in order to successfully implement the company's strategy.

7.2 Cross-selling (C10)

7.2.1 THE VALUE OF RELATIONSHIPS

Price drivers C3, C4, C5, and C6 depart from the perspective of the transaction. In the analysis of the price-to-value ratio, the relationship with the customer, however, barely comes into it. But this relationship does feature explicitly in the tenth price driver: cross-selling (C10). Cross-selling as a sales strategy is not out to maximize profit from one transaction, but instead tries to attract customers with a view to making money off them through multiple transactions. Price is used as bait, and therefore less related to value, costs, or market price: it is based on what the salesperson can earn from the relationship. Given that customers often need more than one purchase to fill a need, this sales technique is widely used and as old as the hills.

In modern times, it was King Camp Gillette who demonstrated the power of cross-selling as a revenue model. King was an anti-capitalist who pursued utopian socialism his whole life. He was also an inventor, and really hit the big time at the age of forty when he came up with the idea for the disposable razor blade. After earlier less successful attempts, his big breakthrough came when he started charging a low price for the razors. This allowed Gillette to generate enormous recurring revenue from the sale of disposal blades. By 1910, this had made him so rich that he moved in circles where he rubbed shoulders with the likes of Henry Ford and Theodore Roosevelt. He turned to them for support in putting his utopian ideals into practice. But contrary to his business exploits, he was less successful in politics.[57]

There are four different ways of applying cross-selling:
1. Split solutions
2. Simple basic version
3. Broad range
4. Bundling

7.2.2 SPLIT SOLUTIONS

This involves selling a product or service in two parts that are both required to meet a need. One part of the split solution is then sold cheaply to attract customers, as Gillette did with his razors. The other part can then be sold at a relatively high price: the blades.

Another contemporary example is Nespresso. Prices of Nespresso coffee machines are low (from €50). Real espresso machines are hundreds of euros more expensive. But a Nespresso machine only works with special Nespresso capsules. And in 2012, these sold for between €0.33 and €0.37 a piece. That makes one cup of Nespresso more expensive than a real espresso: the price of the coffee beans needed for one cup of coffee from an espresso machine ranges from €0.04 to €0.24, depending on brand and quality.[58] As you would expect, Nespresso claims that the coffee in its capsules is of superior quality.[59] But still, the primary aim behind the price of the capsules seems to be to maximize profits generated thanks to customer loyalty. On average, customers spend €80 a month on capsules.[60] The variable costs of capsules customers fork out for every year is therefore approximately one thousand euros. Good-quality coffee beans for an espresso machine are available for an average price of €0.14 per cup of coffee. These variable costs add up to around four hundred euros per annum. That makes an espresso machine six hundred euros a year cheaper to use. By charging a premium on the coffee, Nespresso is able to recoup costs that go into keeping its coffee makers cheap in no time, even after deduction of the costs of a global advertising campaign starring George Clooney.

There are many more examples of split solutions. Mobile telephony operators give away free phones to secure revenue from voice, data, and other services through long-term contracts. Amazon offers customers a Kindle tablet at a low price to be able to sell more e-books, music, and other electronic content to them.

In B2B markets, cross-selling is a rather more nuanced undertaking. Business customers tend to be more conscientious buyers, scrutinizing all aspects of their procurement outlay based on a TCO calculation. TCO stands for total cost of ownership: buyers assess costs across the full period of usage. The cross-selling revenue model will then fall short relatively quickly. Business customers will ask Nespresso for discounts on capsules to bring total cost of ownership into line with alternative solutions.

Still, providers of services and products to business customers are managing to create major additional revenue by selling split solutions. Car leasing firms, IT service providers, photocopier vendors, and other service companies sell long-term contracts based on a volume estimated by the customer at a keen per-unit price. During the term of the contract, volume often turns out higher than estimated, such as in the case of a leased car doing more miles than expected or a photocopier making more copies than the customer thought he would need. The vendor will then capitalize on that by charging the same unit price for excess volume, while unit costs will be lower due to economies of scale. Lower volume than estimated, on the other hand, will entitle the customer to a relatively small discount on the total invoice amount. And that while costs of execution will be significantly lower when volume is lower. This way, the provider always achieves an extra margin when actual volume differs from estimated volume.

7.2.3 SIMPLE BASIC VERSION

As part of this form of cross-selling, the vendor will offer a simple and cheap basic version of a product or service. The underlying aim is to subsequently sell the customer a more comprehensive and expensive solution. Customers will generally first try out the basic version. If they are happy with the product, they may decide to upgrade.

The use of freemium pricing has really taken off in the world of software and Internet services over the past decade. Internet games are free, but as you play them, you may want extras that will cost you. Skype offers free Internet-based telephony, but charges you for group video calling. Sharing pictures on Flickr is free, but additional GBs of storage space for your photos is not.

Akin to offering the option of upgrading after trying out a service is to arouse customers' interest through a basic service. A manufacturer or store will then advertise a low *from* price for a stripped-down basic service. Once this has drawn the customer into the store or show-room, he or she will eventually purchase a more expensive version that better meets his or her needs. In the automotive industry this kind of basic version is referred to as an entry-level model. Nearly every single car ad touts an irresistibly low from price. But the specs of an entry-level model are not very attractive. Popular options are not included and the price does not include any dealer fees. Customers will eventually end up buying a more expensive version. The advertised low price of the entry-level model is an eye-catcher that gives customers the impression that the model is *within reach.*

In the travel industry, from prices are also a favored advertising ingredient. One week at a luxury five-star all-inclusive resort, including flights, for 499 euros? Yes, but only in low season, not during school holidays, when booking six months ahead, and using a quadruple room, otherwise the price will be higher.

7.2.4 **BROAD RANGE — LOSS LEADERS**

This tactic sees the provider communicate a low price for a popular product to attract as much attention as possible. After the low price has served its purpose and generated footfall, the salesman will try to sell other products from his broad range to these customers.

Major accountancy firms, for example, do not only base their revenue model on the invoice they submit to companies for their annual audit. They also sell other services, such as tax advice, transactional support, management consultancy or auditing services to their business relations at CFO level.

In B2B markets it is common practice to submit a low price proposal for the first project. Contractors, facility management providers, and IT service providers will often choose to submit a low price offer just to get their foot in the door. As their relationship with that client endures, they gradually increase their share of wallet[*] by selling this client other services from their portfolio.

Department stores and supermarkets are masters at selling loss leaders at extremely low prices in the hope that, once in their stores, customers will do all their shopping there. Many marketing campaigns that offer you something for nothing are inspired by the hope that you will turn into a regular customer and purchase more products and services.

7.2.5   BUNDLING

Price bundling is a special kind of cross-selling. The previous cross-selling tactics all consisted of companies using a low price to lure in customers in order to then sell them other products and services. In the case of price bundling, however, companies draw attention to the great value customers get when purchasing a combination of goods that the seller has bundled together instead of offering a steep discount on the first purchase alone. Price bundling has the same dynamics as a volume discount (refer to Section 5.4).

The objective of price bundling is to raise revenue. Cable companies, for example, will often bundle Internet, phone, and TV together and sell these packages for a fixed monthly fee. This is cross-selling of Internet and phone, alongside the traditional offering of TV channels.

7.2.6   COMPLEXITY OF ANALYSIS

The pricing analysis for cross-selling is complex. It requires assessment of demand at various price levels for multiple products and services. The individual products and services appeal to different customers and customer segments. They each have their own specific competition landscape. The attractiveness of interlinked offers to customers is consequently not the sum of the individual products.

---

[*] Share of wallet: the share of a customer's budget that they spend on your product or service. A facility services provider, for example, cleans a building for €10,000. Their customer's total facility costs amount to €100,000. That makes facility service provider's share of wallet 10%: an opportunity to gain 90%.

Results of cross-selling are difficult to predict or evaluate. And comparing the effectiveness of two forms of this tactic is also quite a challenge. Defining and applying these kinds of pricing models requires a great deal of commercial experience.

7.3 Co-selling (C11)

7.3.1 NETWORK RELATIONSHIPS

Contrary to cross-selling (C10), the focus of co-selling (C11) is not on relationships with customers, but on relationships with third parties. Co-selling thrives in a network. A manufacturer can make money out of other parties in a network by offering certain groups cheap or even free services. A simple form of co-selling is a B2B supplier who sells services to his client's employees, which are paid for by the employer.

The C11 price driver is particularly relevant when the parties involved are far removed from each other. Most advertisers do not traditionally have a relationship with users of Internet companies such as Facebook or Google. These Internet powerhouses offer their web services for free. And they subsequently sell advertisers access to their users through co-selling. Co-selling is one of the driving forces behind the Internet economy (more about this later). On numerous websites, consumers "pay" for the service with their attention.

Still, co-selling was around long before the Internet started its ascent. Just think about how often people give someone a benefit in order to curry favor with a third party. Commercial television and complex infrastructure projects are examples from the traditional economy. Commercial TV channels let consumers watch for free, while advertisers pay. Influential environmental pressure groups have the power to curb the progress of major infrastructure projects, such as for oil drilling or the construction of motorways or railways. "Free" additions such as a wildlife crossing are an effective way of ensuring construction and exploitation of the motorway can continue unimpeded.

7.3.2 CO-SELLING AND THE INTERNET

Co-selling has taken off online in the way that it has thanks to the Internet's unique structure of cost and value.[61] Certain costs are considerably lower online. And the Internet also enables forms of value creation that entrepreneurs never even dared dream of before 1990.

First off, we will look at factors that are making the cost function incomparable. Next, we will go into the unique online sources of value creation.

7.3.3 LOWER COSTS ONLINE

Costs can traditionally be allocated to four sources:
- Design and creation — "R&D"
- Production and raw materials — "factory"
- Delivery — "logistics"
- Marketing and sales — "sales & marketing"

A company's R&D department designs the products. It compiles specifications and submits these to procurement, production, and assembly for execution. Design and production come with significant cost. The company launches marketing campaigns, while its account managers visit customers. Supply chain management sees to it that the physical goods are delivered.

Online costs, on the other hand, sometimes stem from only one source: design and creation. Costs from the other three sources are as good as negligible. We will outline how the Internet makes these costs "disappear" in the following order:
a. Production
b. Delivery
c. Marketing and sales

a. Production
In traditional industries, more sales mean higher costs for production, raw materials, and delivery. Online, the variable costs of serving users ("production") are nearly zero. All that is needed to absorb a

growing user base is server space. Data centers are cheap and costs will drop over time. Therefore the only significant production costs that an Internet company incurs are one-time costs for the design and creation of the application. This requires an effort in writing the code for the software.

b. Delivery
The costs involved in providing an Internet service are low and flexible. Besides, both bandwidth from the data center to the cloud and connectivity for users are becoming ever cheaper.

c. Marketing and sales
Marketing and sales costs are low. In offline sectors, it can be quite expensive to advertise for customers. Satisfied users of Internet services, however, bring in new users with great ease, quickly, and for free. Word-of-mouth advertising for a good website happens both offline and online. Google has made billions of dollars from its search services without spending anything on marketing. Attracting customers and sales to advertisers can be virtually free.

7.3.4 HIGHER VALUE ONLINE

Value creation traditionally primarily happens through the seller's proposition. The low cost of doing business online now offers unprecedented opportunities of combining users and services in a way that will boost value. In the following, we will go into four sources of additional value creation:
a. Transparency
b. Modularity
c. Unlimited supply ("long tail")
d. Network

a. Transparent
Easy access ("one click away") and the absence of geographical obstacles ("virtual") make it easy to quickly form a perception of a website's value. The quality of providers can be verified by checking blogs, taking part in chat sessions, or through other forms of communication across the enormous Internet community. Transparency

also concerns the price. Price comparison websites force providers to give some serious thought to how they can differentiate themselves from the competition.

b. Modular ("link")

Traditionally, companies compete with each other. They want to provide the most comprehensive service possible to their customers. Internet-based companies, however, like to supplement each other in order to help customers, either through formal partnerships and affiliate marketing programs or otherwise. Sites often use links to refer users to applications that can meet a specific need. Providers are increasingly specializing in their own area. When an Internet company has become the leader in a specific market segment, it will after a while often end up serving the vast majority of that market (winner takes all). Websites that do not offer a certain feature themselves will link users to the dominant and most developed website in that specific market segment.

c. Unlimited supply ("long tail")

There are few limitations to the online presentation of a product range. The assortment can be changed at any time of the day. In principle, the number of goods or services that can be offered is endless. Traditional sales channels that present products in showrooms and shops are confined to the physical floor space they have available. Sales staff often has a catalogue and price book that are periodically updated. The extra range that can be presented online is known as the Internet's long tail. One single item from the long tail will create relatively little revenue. But Internet-based companies will still have tapped a considerable source of revenue, as they can offer a nigh on unlimited assortment.

d. Network value

As soon as an Internet company has conquered its niche through differentiating quality, it will create a large network of users. The huge and global scope of Facebook and Skype were unthinkable back in 1990. For that reason alone, these networks in themselves are already valuable, because a social media user wants to be part of the largest networks. After all, that will give him or her more contacts, as well as the opportunity to strike up more connections than elsewhere. And those people who were already using the network are also winners, because the influx of new users means they always have new users with whom they can communicate. At the end of the day, all Facebook users benefit from using one and the same network instead of posting their photos and messages on ten different networks.

 ## 7.4 Cohesion (C12)

7.4.1 BALANCE

Cohesion (C12) is the last price driver in our review of the art of pricing. This is not a stand-alone price driver, but instead one that emphasizes the need for balance between the other eleven price drivers. Cohesion requires the well-honed skills of a true pricing manager. Creativity, intuition and experience are what's needed.

7.4.2 EXAMPLE: THE AIRLINE INDUSTRY

A fine example of the power of cohesion can be found in the airline industry, where traditional airlines maintain networks of routes. This section will first look at the pricing techniques these network airlines use. Despite using many price drivers to optimize revenue from their networks, their financial results are almost always poor. We will therefore compare them to another category of providers, the so-called low-cost carriers. What becomes apparent is that there is insufficient cohesion between price drivers at traditional airlines.

Traditional airlines increase the number of routes they can sell by striking up strategic alliances with airlines in other parts of the world or through acquisitions of other airlines (C2). The value they provide hinges on a timetable that is predictable to customers, good service on board their aircraft, and great concern for safety (C3). For each customer segment and for each route, they pay a price that matches the value provided. On routes where there is little competition, they generally charge higher fares (C4). They also use price customization (C5) in a range of different ways, such as:

- based on the time and place of booking and the flight, with lower fares for passengers who book their flights early and by charging a premium for flights at sought-after times;
- based on customer segment, by giving a discount to holidaymakers, for example;
- based on the number of flights purchased, which can see an airline give a volume discount to companies;
- based on product and service, as reflected in the distinction between economy class and business class, for example;
- based on distribution channel, by giving discounts to tour operators and agents (online and offline).

Airlines also offer services related to flying, such as hotel accommodation and car rental, while selling a varied range of goods on the actual flights (C10). And they pioneered the concept of loyalty schemes, awarding business travelers popular frequent flyer miles to coax them into flying with them as much as possible, while the employer pays for the (more expensive) tickets (C11).

The traditional airlines are convinced that price drivers help them make a profit. They have, especially when compared to other industries, large pricing departments that are often manned by hundreds of employees. They are particularly enthusiastic about price driver C5, price customization. Former American Airlines CEO Robert Crandall once said: "If I've got 2,000 customers on any given route and 400 different fares, I'm clearly still 1,600 fares short".[62] American Airlines pioneered the kind of complex revenue management and pricing systems that were later copied by all major traditional network airlines.

But how well are these airlines actually performing? Profitability across the industry has traditionally always been low.[63] In the US, the airline business as a whole made a cumulative *loss* of $2 billion between 1947 and 1991. There were some signs of a recovery at the end of the 1990s, but by 2005 the cumulative result from 1947 was negative again, both in nominal and real terms.[*] The long-term fi-

---

[*] Nominal: effects of inflation have not been factored in. Real: effects of inflation have been factored in.

nancial performance of this industry, which has been a major driving force behind the development of advanced pricing, more than any other industry, are so poor that unquestioningly following their methods may not be such a good idea.

Over the decades following American Airlines' introduction of revenue management, a second business model for airlines emerged. Southwest Airlines and Transavia were the first successful low-cost carriers. Many so-called no-frills airlines are profitable and generate above-average growth thanks to low prices. They manage to keep fares down through, for example, low costs of an efficient fleet, limited service, and cheaper staff.

One critical factor underlying the success of low-cost airlines is the complexity reduction they have accomplished in processes and operations. When it comes to pricing, they limit themselves to the forms of price customization that matter most to them. They simply do not bother with other forms of customizing fares.

Around the year 2000, low-cost airlines were the first to start selling all their fares online, achieving unprecedented levels of fare transparency and purchasing convenience. The network airlines, on the other hand, still had confusing websites that would initially not reveal their cheapest fares to online shoppers.

Low-cost carriers customize fares based on the time of booking and supplementary services. A fare will be higher if more people have already booked a seat on the flight in question. And supplementary services are charged separately. There are surcharges on top of the fare for services such as additional luggage allowance, reserving a specific seat or drinks and snacks on the flight. The time of booking and supplementary services are two essential dimensions for low-cost carriers that allow them to assess willingness to pay and cost to serve across their market. This way, they can create the desired price image in customers' perception by advertising a very low from price, while simultaneously generating sufficient revenue through more expensive tickets.

Traditional airlines simply cannot match this kind of simplicity. They use complex fare structures and conditions such as a minimum stay, advanced purchase, booking classes with different rules for changing or cancelling a ticket and corresponding fees, frequent flyer schemes for passengers, loyalty schemes for companies, upgrade options, lounge access, priority lanes, corporate discounts, and other schemes aimed at attaining "optimum" price customization. Not only have traditional airlines proven to be insufficiently capable of reducing complexity (C9), the very way they work also leads to more costs (C6). By taking differentiation between customers to such an extreme in selling and executing flights, they are increasing their costs. And traditional airlines are also deficient in the area of fairness (C7). Although CEO Crandall of American Airlines would not be satisfied until he had 2,000 different fares for 2,000 passengers, most travelers are not amused when they find out there is a large difference between what they paid for a ticket and what the person next to them on the plane paid; they may also think that the fare depends on (too) many different factors.

The network airlines have overshot the mark in their application of pricing methods. Their pricing policy is hampered by a lack of cohesion (C12) between the price drivers of customization (C5), costs (C6), communication (C7), and complexity reduction (C9).

7.4.3 EXAMPLE: INTERNET COMPANIES

High-profile Internet companies such as Facebook, LinkedIn, Twitter, Google, and Spotify have managed to amass a network of users and become dominant in their respective niches within a short time span. They all provide services for free. The success of their revenue model hinges on cohesion (C12) between cross-selling (C10) and co-selling (C11) on the one hand and the opportunities that the Internet's unique structure of cost (C6) and value (C3) offers on the other hand.

Google's search engine is free to use. They sell adverts based on the search terms users enter (C11). Adverts tie in with an acute need of a potential customer. An advert will appear at a very relevant moment, namely when a consumer enters a specific search term. This relevance is the true value (C3) that enables higher fees for Google ads based on co-selling.

LinkedIn sells valuable advertising space, as it enables the advertiser to select where to advertise based on the user's professional domain and location (C3, C11). Business services providers can hence get in contact with interested employees at their clients. An IT provider from India can reach CIOs in countries where it intends to increase its market share. Also, LinkedIn lets professionals post a profile with a CV for free. They do charge, however, for options such as sending messages (InMails) to potential employers or clients (C10).

Facebook lets advertisers select where to advertise based on detailed personal characteristics (C11). The value Facebook offers its users is very high. Users spend a lot of time on Facebook and the number of users has grown rapidly. Revenue from ads, however, has been disappointing so far; users seem to take little notice of adverts on Facebook. Cohesion (C12) between Facebook's customer value (C3) and advertising revenue (C11) is therefore seen as not yet being optimal. Obviously, this status at the beginning of 2013 may very well change in the years to follow.

Spotify offers free unlimited (C3) online music streaming with commercial breaks. If you want to listen to music online without adverts, you will be charged 5 euros a month. For a monthly fee of 10 euros, you can also do so offline (C10). Spotify has developed modular value by entering into an alliance with Facebook (C11). Facebook friends can share the music they are listening to on Spotify. Users benefit from simple and valuable suggestions for songs and bands from people they know.

7.4.4 IN CLOSING

We have now reviewed the twelve price drivers you need to take into account when designing a revenue model and setting your prices. This naturally leads to the question of how best to determine the price and which price drivers carry most significance for any specific type of company. The answer to that question lies in the nature of art.

Selecting price drivers is an art: the art of the true entrepreneur who chooses a strategy, business model, and price drivers, and creates a corporate culture, that best suit the objectives of this enterprise, as well as himself as a person. Objectively choosing the best price driver is therefore not possible. You can compare this to style choices made throughout the history of painting: Dutch masters in the seventeenth century based their style choices on considerations that differed from those used by Karel Appel in the twentieth century, who basically threw some paint at a canvas using brushes, filling knives, and his bare hands. And in that same vein, the value-driven pricing methods deployed by German car manufacturers are wasted on Facebook and Google, who are changing the world by making valuable services available for free and unlimited in exchange for user details and attention.

In this part, the central focus was always on the *level* of prices, while we paid relatively little attention to the *basis* of prices (the pricing model). This was a conscious choice, aimed at keeping the explanation as simple and accessible as possible. However, selection of a pricing model is subject to the same twelve price drivers we discussed in this part of the book. Note: in industries such as software, (public) transport, telecommunications, and publishing, the basis of a price has such considerable influence that it cannot be considered separately from the level of a price. For a taxi company, for example, the choice between a fixed fee per journey, a per-minute rate, or a per-mile rate is a fundamental one; the same goes for software companies, which can opt for a licensing-based model or a subscription model.

In the preceding chapters we covered the twelve considerations that determine the price and pricing model. In the next part, we will go into the methods available to us to, after having selected one or multiple price drivers, set the best possible prices.

PART II

The science of pricing

Layer 1
Expert Judgment

Layer 2
Implicit Measurement

Layer 3
Explicit Measurement

Price Sensitivity

CHAPTER 8

Substantiation

8.1 Both an art and a science

Part I showed that the art of pricing is a creative process. But the substantiation of pricing takes us into the realm of science, the science of pricing. Pricing is both an art and a science: art qualifies, science quantifies. The art is all about choosing a pricing strategy and revenue model. The science identifies and substantiates the optimum price level, based on price drivers. The science "provides the figures" and validates the selection of the revenue model and strategy. This second part of the book is about the scientific side of pricing.

The selection of a business model and price drivers determines what kind of research is required to set optimum prices. Information about cost structure and procurement costs in the market will be most valued by a manufacturer who intends to conquer the global market through cost leadership (C2, C4, and C6). And if you want to set and customize your prices based on perceived value among your target group and the variety of individual needs (C3, C5), your pricing research will primarily have to be about customer perception and value.

8.2 Price sensitivity and research

The core question of pricing research is:

- How high is demand for your product or service with certain prices or pricing structures?

Asking people about their price sensitivity or willingness to pay* is by no means straightforward, as there are many factors at play.

Direct questions about the effects of price changes provide little information. There are several reasons for that. Consumers and buyers often do not know the answer or give an answer that contradicts their actual behavior. And respondents are sometimes also not prepared to reveal at what price they would proceed to purchase a product or service. Aside from that, their price sensitivity will change as circumstances, such as the competition's prices, change.

Empirical research into the impact of price changes consisting of observing consumers' behavior instead of directly asking them questions also comes with all sorts of complicating factors. The large number of mutual dependencies makes it hard to predict the effect of the price. A price cut, for example, will have an effect on customers, but also on competitors. And that response by competitors will, in turn, change the effect the initial price cut had on customers. A reduction in sales following an increase in prices can have a side effect of higher costs as production is scaled down. But higher prices can also reflect positively on a company in terms of its image and hence on rare occasions even increase sales.

In practice, many commercial managers consequently prefer to ignore price research and tools. They mistrust the evangelists who push price research, tools, and consultancy services. That mistrust is partly justified. Blind faith in the results of price research will make a one-eyed man king.

---

* Price sensitivity is fluctuation in demand following price changes. Willingness to pay is the maximum price a customer is willing to pay for a product or service. Insight into the relation between demand and price will lead to understanding of these two variables.

Still, the benefits of a data-driven approach are considerable, if you only manage to come up with a well thought-out combination of research, existing information, practical experience, and the creativity of a pricing strategy. The factual basis produced by research provides a common ground for all stakeholders. This will inspire new ideas for better prices. And this is also how simple shortcomings in pricing will be laid bare.

This low-hanging fruit offers a prime opportunity for a profit boost. After all, a price change is a profit lever. A minor improvement to a price of only a few percentage points will propel a far greater percentage rise in profit.[*]

8.3   FirstPrice Pricing Funnel

The multi-tier approach of the FirstPrice Pricing Funnel (FPF) enables optimum utilization of information about price sensitivity, weighing up costs, workability, and attention from management. The most detailed studies, software, and tools are set aside for the biggest challenges. The FPF recognizes the moment when more in-depth research of more accurate information will produce greater yields. Methods for more in-depth research result in greater precision and reliability, but they are also more expensive and labor-intensive.

Without pricing science, a company will lack structural knowledge about price sensitivity. The sales organization or marketing department will then have neither indicative information nor implicit know-how to fall back on. Customers' reactions to prices are not considered a pertinent focus point by the commercial organization. Of course, there is always the odd person who ventures an opinion about price and supposed customer responses at internal policy meetings. But this is not a structural operation. Nobody is in a position to be able to judge whether these kinds of opinions actually wash. Sometimes (external) research broaches the subject of price, but the methodological underpinning is generally weak.

[*]   Refer to Chapter 2

Unfortunately, many companies still have not got past this stage. There is no clear and unequivocal allocation of pricing responsibilities. Price is a subject that everyone weighs in on, but no one takes responsibility for.

The FirstPrice Pricing Funnel (FPF) offers a point of reference for the development and retention of knowledge about price sensitivity (see Figure 10). The funnel has three layers containing all possible information about prices, price sensitivity, and underlying factors.

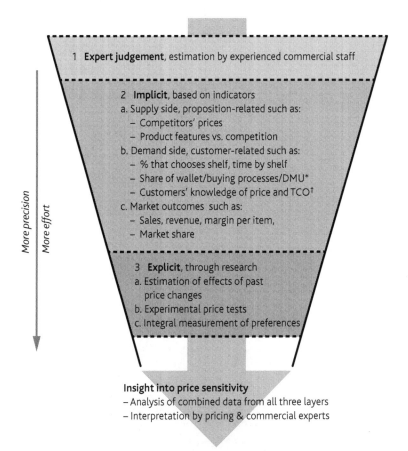

1 **Expert judgement**, estimation by experienced commercial staff

2 **Implicit**, based on indicators
a. Supply side, proposition-related such as:
   – Competitors' prices
   – Product features vs. competition
b. Demand side, customer-related such as:
   – % that chooses shelf, time by shelf
   – Share of wallet/buying processes/DMU*
   – Customers' knowledge of price and TCO†
c. Market outcomes such as:
   – Sales, revenue, margin per item,
   – Market share

3 **Explicit**, through research
a. Estimation of effects of past price changes
b. Experimental price tests
c. Integral measurement of preferences

More precision
More effort

Insight into price sensitivity
– Analysis of combined data from all three layers
– Interpretation by pricing & commercial experts

Figure 10 The FirstPrice Pricing Funnel yields insight into price sensitivity with optimum alignment of efforts, precision, and methods

* DMU: decision making unit, the people who decide whether or not to purchase
† TCO: total cost of ownership, i.e. the total costs of purchase and usage to fulfill a need over a certain period of time

8.3.1 EXPERT JUDGMENT

Expert judgment is the first layer of the FPF. It forms the basis for a fact-based approach to pricing at a company. This layer channels the experience and intuition of subject matter experts and makes their assessments explicit. The subject matter experts are commercial professionals and employees with (partial) responsibility for price. In their day-to-day activities, they develop beliefs based on which they evaluate customers' choices and the role of the price.

8.3.2 IMPLICIT MEASUREMENT

The second layer is that of implicit measurement. What we measure here are key price-related variables in customers' decision-making. This leads to an implicit estimation of price sensitivity and willingness to pay. One oil company, for example, has decided to follow the market leader whenever it changes its prices (C8). In doing so, the oil company has set up an information system that closely tracks price fluctuations at the market leader. In their market, which is one where players follow the price leader, these are crucial indicators.

8.3.3 EXPLICIT MEASUREMENT

Explicit measurement is the third layer. This is research aimed at unearthing correlations between demand, price, supply, and market factors that impact on price sensitivity. The ambition is to model all relevant factors and thus make an explicit estimation of price sensitivity based on knowledge of the entire system.

8.3.4 USING THE FUNNEL

When setting prices, managers are often partly led by a subconscious judgment of price sensitivity. Practical experience has given them expertise on this issue, as they are generally the ones experiencing the fallout of price changes. The first layer of expert judgment is utilized by making this subconscious judgment explicit and lifting it into conscious awareness.

These same managers often already draw on a wide variety of management information that also implicitly suggests price sensitivity levels. Utilization of the indicators of the second layer hence quickly comes within reach. When interpreted carefully, existing data sources and reports can provide useful indications about price sensitivity.

Explicit measurements from the third layer offer help in case of major uncertainties or great impact of a decision. This kind of research departs from initial insights from layer 1 and 2, and checks assumptions against more elaborate data.

The FPF filters a reliable price sensitivity estimation through three layers. This approach enables prioritization within a large number of prices for different products and markets and segments.

This second part of the book provides an overview of pricing research and information across the three layers of the FPF. We will outline the procedures and methods for each layer. Examples will help to manifest the purpose and limitations of all methods.

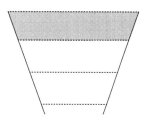

CHAPTER 9
Expert judgment (layer 1)

9.1 Making beliefs explicit

Beliefs about price sensitivity have a great impact on pricing decisions. They are the product of experience in the trade or acquired
doctrines. Not only the price level, but also the selection of price
drivers and revenue model draws on these beliefs, which are often
not 100% conscious beliefs.

When commercial managers depart from the idea that "customers
want the lowest price", they will base their decisions on the market
price principle and pass over the price driver of customer value (C3).
And when a financial director has learnt in university that a "fair"
selling price is made up of the average cost price plus a "healthy"
profit mark-up, his preferred principle is that of cost price. He will
not be aware of customer value (C3).

The first layer of the pricing funnel converts beliefs into quantitative
statements about prices, making the beliefs explicit and quantifiable.
This conversion produces the possibility of testing out the expected
effects of a pricing policy. This exercise lets managers at a company
share the principles on which they base their pricing decisions. An

explicit discussion about assumptions is a good starting point for the development of a better revenue model.

The most important changes in pricing and strategy are propelled by newly acquired awareness. Imagine a situation where an entrepreneur provides added value to a specific customer group in the market. The entrepreneur, however, will only change his (pricing) policy when he really *becomes convinced* that the value he adds enfranchises him to charge a higher price in this niche market.

The first layer of the FPF is the one that is least driven by data. Internal experts' judgment arises from informal working methods. Introducing structure into these methods will bring overview and transparency, which will, in turn, improve price evaluations. That would, for example, enable structural recording of price sensitivity estimations. The commercial team will then make a formal estimation of the number of items sold at a price that is 10% higher. The expected effects of a price cut and price rise on profits, sales, and market share will subsequently be easy to deduce. Discussing the issued prognoses will make beliefs and price drivers transparent.

Concrete and explicit estimations of changes in sales following a price change serve two goals. Team members will first experience how certain or uncertain they are about the effects of price changes. This will lay the basis from which further efforts can be launched in gathering data and measuring price sensitivity in layers 2 and 3 of the FPF. Secondly, these estimations enable us to better assess the expected possibilities offered by better prices. The team members will then soon become aware of the power of price based on their own estimations. That will make it easier to gain broad support both for day-to-day pricing decisions and for initiatives aimed at strengthening the pricing function.

9.2 Example of a team exercise

9.2.1 INPUT

This example will revolve around a pricing manager who applies the first layer of the FPF for the attractively priced eMove base smartphone (€159). This phone is the popular entry-level model marketed by an up-and-coming telephone manufacturer from China.

The pricing manager at head office contacts the local team of five employees in the Netherlands, which boasts excellent knowledge of the market and is in charge of implementing the pricing policy. He asks them to make two simple estimations. Each team member is to state by what percentage he or she thinks sales will fluctuate following a €10 price cut and a €10 price rise.

eMove base. % sales fluctuation – 2 scenarios

		Sales volume 2012: 200,000	Revenue 2012: €20,555,915	Retail price 1: €149	Retail price 2: €169
Expert 1	Jan	Product mngr		8%	–5%
Expert 2	Maaike	Jr prod mngr		6%	–6%
Expert 3	Rob	Planning		5%	–7%
Expert 4	Quirine	Sales mngr		10%	–10%
Expert 5	Joop	Market research		6%	–7%

Table 6 Estimations by the five subject matter experts at the local sales organization of a smartphone manufacturer (fictitious data).

When the pricing manager shows the chart with the estimations to the team, they all agree that there is little difference between their estimations (see Table 6). Four of the subject matter experts expect a €10 price cut to lead to a sales hike of between 5% and 8%. They think sales will drop by 5% to 7% when the price is raised by €10. Only Quirine, the sales manager, thinks the impact on sales will be greater, estimating it at 10%.

Figure 11 offsets the team's expected sales fluctuations against seven price points. The sales volume at the current retail price of €159 equals the actual volume of 200,000 items for 2012. With a price of either €149 or €169, the forecast based on the input given will apply. The other price points (€144, €154, €164, and €174) were filled in using linear interpolation. Sales volume at €154 is the average of the volume at €149 and at €159.

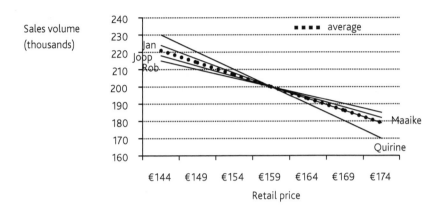

Figure 11 Expected relationship between sales volume and price based on each team member's input (fictitious data)

9.2.2 EXPLICIT REVENUE EXPECTATIONS

The pricing manager at the smartphone maker then goes on to assess the effects of the price changes on profits and revenue. Based on the answers to two questions he makes the most important financial implications as expected by the team explicit.

Figure 12 depicts the relationship between price and revenue as foreseen by each team member. The dotted line denotes the "average", that is to say the joint prognosis of all team members. The team expects changes in price to only have a minor effect on revenue, hence the relatively flat average line.

The difference in revenue at the two prices at the extremes of the scale, €144 and €174, is below 5%. Considering the relatively big margins for error we are working with in the first layer of the pricing funnel, 5% is a small difference.

Figure 12 Expected correlation between manufacturer's revenue and price (fictitious data, 19% VAT, and 30% markup for retailer)

9.2.3 EXPLICIT PROFIT EXPECTATIONS

After a cost analysis based on internal financial data, the pricing manager visualizes the impact on profits. He calculates impact on the joint prognosis for prices between €149 and €169. The lever effect of price on profits really comes to the fore here.

The team foresees a significant rise in profits (between 10% and 15%) when the price is higher (see Figure 13).

Figure 13 Expected correlation between profits and price (fictitious data, 19% VAT, 30% markup for retailer, 15% markup for manufacturer at a price of €159, ratio of fixed to variable costs is 50% at a price of €159)

The pricing manager has made this joint belief explicit and transparent. His proposals for price changes subsequently receive greater attention. The results spark a discussion about the opportunities offered by a better pricing policy.

The pricing manager proceeds by making a research plan describing what additional data needs to be collected and analyzed and how. This research shall better map price sensitivity and provide the team and the pricing manager with foundations for a final decision about new prices.

The next two chapters will go into which data and methods will give the team greater insight into price sensitivity. Chapter 10 will discuss indicative data. This is the FPF's second layer, implicit measurement. Integrated methods, or the FPF's third layer of explicit measurement, will be covered in Chapter 11.

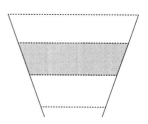

CHAPTER 10

Implicit measurement (layer 2)

10.1 Introduction

The second layer of detail of the FPF is based on implicit measurement. This layer comprises indicators about price sensitivity, giving the decision maker a better idea of correlations between price, demand, revenue, and profit.

One example of an indicator from the second layer of the FPF is market share. A change in market share may mirror customers' response to a price change. This information is indicative only, as market share not only depends on pricing, but also on other factors, such as the attractiveness of products and services, the level of competition, and developments in distribution channels.

Implicit measurement is easy to do, because companies have lots of commercial data from which to extrapolate relevant indications. This includes data about revenue, sales volume, market shares, competitors' prices, and customer segments. When interpreted correctly, these indicators can be used for implicit research into price sensitivity. Unfortunately, traditional business functions generally fail to make the most of pricing intelligence opportunities based on data they already have available. This is down to the fact that price is only their second priority, as we will see in Chapter 14. For a well-focused pricing function, implicit measurement is the driver that can bring important initial improvements.

The selection, definition, and purpose of indicators differ from one price driver to the next. Revenue models tend to be based on a combination of price drivers. Companies therefore need indicative information that is specific to their strategy. A mobile network operator, for example, could decide to follow the price leader (C8).* The indicators this company will use to gauge the effects of that decision will not be the ones it would use if it were to seek to get across an image of "fairness" through advertising (C7).

Below you will find a chart of indicators that are typically used for each price driver. Although there is also other data that matters, Table 7 lists the indicators that should be looked at first.

Market share, for example, is listed under corporate strategy (C2), while sales volume comes under profitability (C1). Market share and sales volume also provide an indication of the value provided (C3). However, the primary focus for value is on data about the proposition and the value customers ascribe to a product or service.

To what extent data will actually be useful depends on the reliability of the source and method of measurement. Price signaling techniques for tacit collusion (C8) in the airline industry are possible when prices are recorded electronically. For a long time, this was only the case in Western markets. The advent of the Internet has greatly improved reliability of indicators of competitor behavior.

In B2B markets, collecting market prices presents companies with a challenge. An estimation of 3 cents for a one-minute mobile call under an SME† contract will be less reliable when it was made based on two offers from one competitor than when based on an analysis of the top 5 operators' price and discount lists for SMEs.

---

* In price level or in price parameters, such as charging calls by the minute
† SME: Small or Medium sized Enterprise

Price driver		*Indicators*
Performance		
C1	Company profitability	Sales volume, revenue, margin
C2	Corp. strategy & business model	Market data (size, share, growth), furthermore dependent on specific strategy
Transaction		
C3	Customer value	Proposition, value drivers, and valuation by customers
C4	Competition	Prices and pricing structure of competitors
C5	Customization	Customer intelligence
C6	Costs	Costs (fixed/variable, direct/indirect) and cost development
Communication		
C7	Communication to customers	Perception by and behavior of customers in response to communication
C8	Tacit collusion	Behavior of competitors in market
C9	Complexity reduction	Pricing structures, business model
Relationship		
C10	Cross-selling	Relationships between products/services
C11	Co-selling	Relationships between stakeholders

Table 7 Chart of indicators that are typically used for the first 11 price drivers

This chapter will provide an overview of important indicators in three different subdomains:

- Supply side
- Demand side
- Market outcomes

The supply side is about propositions and prices in the market in which your company and your competitors operate. Indicators on the demand side cover customer characteristics and behavior. Market outcomes are transaction-related, emerging when supply meets demand. We will go into implicit measurement of price sensitivity for each of these categories in the upcoming sections.

10.2   Supply side

On the supply side, your and your competitors' propositions and prices determine your success in the market. We will first discuss prices in consumer markets, and then move on to B2B environments. And in closing, we will go over indicators of the value of a proposition.

10.2.1   COMPETITOR PRICES IN RETAIL AND B2C[*]

Prior to setting a price for his product or service, an entrepreneur will have acquired sound knowledge of what's available in his market and at what price. A first look at the market provides an idea that can serve as the starting point for further exploration. He will conduct a detailed comparison of propositions and prices of all providers. His focus will primarily be on those features of propositions that have the biggest impact on customer value.[†]

In case of complex propositions and prices, a structured approach will be needed. Standardization is an important prerequisite for comparability. Diligence in the approach to data will lead to unequivocal and clear conclusions, which is even more important when managers from several departments, such as marketing, sales, strategy, and finance, are involved in the decision-making process.

Each provider will normally have a detailed understanding of their own pricing structure.[‡] Gaining insight into your competitors' prices will therefore present a bigger challenge. Even companies that go by the market price principle,[§] often base themselves on unreliable and unclear information about competitors' prices.

---

[*] B2C: business-to-consumer, companies who produce goods and services for use by end consumers. This book considers retail to be a separate category and not part of B2C, because the retail business model is one of an "intermediary".

[†] These features are the most important *value drivers*, refer to Part I (The Art of pricing)

[‡] Sometimes insight into the company's own prices is also lacking. Prices are too complex (refer to Part I, C9) or there is insufficient focus and prices are left unchanged for years.

[§] Refer to Chapter 2

This subsection will take a closer look at ways of acquiring solid information about competitors' prices in retail and B2C. In the following subsection, we will go into market prices in B2B.

Apples to apples

A competitor analysis will only have real meaning when it compares "apples to apples". A sound analysis will compare prices of largely identical products and services. You can, for example, include brand positioning in the analysis if that has a significant impact on price sensitivity. This is done by using expert judgment to assess brand perception, which will see brand perception classed on a scale of "high, medium, low", or using another form of classification.

In the automotive industry, brand has major influence on consumers' value perception. Brands of the likes of BMW, Mercedes, Audi, Jaguar, Lexus, and Volvo make up the high segment. This brand positioning determines what your peer group is. Peer group members are competitors whose brand positioning is comparable to yours. Prices charged across the peer group are the benchmark indicating the relevant market price. Prices of Audis matter to Lexus, prices of Kias do not. Consistent adherence to the rules and logic of benchmarking will lead to better and faster decisions.

Attention to individual observations

Another requirement for a diligent approach to data is not to "lump all prices together". Before we start calculating and analyzing averages, it pays to take a detailed look at individual observations. The reason for that is twofold. Firstly, sound data analysis may reveal deficiencies, such as individual observations that we are led to mistrust based on experience. Secondly, we are better able to grasp the structure of the market when individual observations chime with the representation of commercial reality. An average smothers understanding of multiple products or companies in one single figure.

Let us explain this with an example: towel prices in the Netherlands, based on fictitious data about the cheapest small-size towel (50x100cm) suppliers. The category manager at a retail chain is in charge of putting together and pricing the towel range at her chain's outlets. As part of her research, she visited stores of five major players at the low end of the Dutch retail market, namely Action, Hema, Blokker, Ikea, and Leen Bakker. The average price for a small towel at these five chains is €2.05.

Closer inspection of the data, however, reveals that Blokker's price is quite a bit out of sync (see Figure 14). The category manager decides not to consider this price in the market analysis. The benchmark average she uses is therefore €1.62. Action and Hema are rather well-placed in the market with their prices of €1.79 and €1.89 respectively, compared to the average market price of €1.62.

Figure 14 Overview of individual competitors' prices based on shop visits for small-size towels 50 x 100 cm (fictitious data)

Looking at *individual* observations instead of only considering the average of €1.62 will enhance our understanding of the structure in the low end of the market. There is a clear distinction between Hema and Action on the one hand, and Leen Bakker and Ikea on the other. Leen Bakker's and Ikea's towels are very keenly priced. Close analysis would then have to show whether they use price drivers such as good-better-best pricing (C7), cross-selling (C10), or cost leadership (C2). Prices at Hema and Action now seem quite a bit higher. Those at Leen Bakker and Ikea are about 25% lower. The conclusion the category manager arrives at when basing herself on individual observations differs from the conclusion based on the average market price.

The importance of careful observation and accurate analysis may seem self-evident, but is often not taken as such in practice. Employees misinterpreting a competitor's retail price or offer is a regular occurrence. Spreadsheets for pricing analysis will subsequently perform incorrect operations using the data entered, leading to commercial managers not having all propositions available to them for their assessment of the market.

In the above example of the price of a specific size towel, the analysis is trivial. In reality, retail chains such as Blokker, Hema, and Ikea need large numbers of such analyses. Errors will then soon go unnoticed. Deviations from the pricing strategy due to poor implementation lead to a loss of revenue and margin.

In our example, the quality of the analysis is all the more important to Action, providing this company's strategy is to always use low prices. Based on the average market price of €2.05, Action can safely keep its price at €1.79. But closer analysis of each observation prompts a price cut down to €1.39. Simply improving the execution of a relatively straightforward analysis will therefore necessitate a price cut by as much as 22%, which has major consequences for sales volume, revenue, and margin.

Online prices and pricebots

The meteoric rise of e-commerce has greatly benefited price transparency. It is far easier to compare prices online than to go out and visit shops to check their prices. Airlines have traditionally been using computer-operated comparisons of competitors' prices through flight reservation systems. And the travel industry was therefore one of the frontrunners in terms of industries that started using pricebots.

Pricebots are computer programs for automated price collection. These robots monitor price distances, alerting the user to every price change in the market. There are companies who automatically change their price based on such an alert. Pricebots are increasingly used by retailers and e-tailers.[*]

---

[*] e-tailers are online retailers

10.2.2 COMPETITOR PRICES IN B2B

Competitor prices are trickier to get hold of in B2B markets. Salespeople only reveal their prices to customers and prospects. Prices and discounts are considered confidential information, and finding out what they are requires considerable effort. This section will focus on four sources that can be used to get an accurate idea of market prices:

1. Price and discount lists
2. Customized offers
3. Win/loss data
4. External research firms

1. Price and discount lists

Price lists in B2B generally present *list prices* or *gross prices*. These are subject to volume discounts and other conditions. When a provider does not publish a list of prices and discounts on its website, a personal approach will be the only way of finding out what these prices and discounts are.

Account managers find out information about competitors during talks with customers. Customers will sometimes refer to price lists or discount lists of competitors, or perhaps even be able to provide a copy of such lists. Customers' reason for doing that may be that they want to insert transparency into the process. Information obtained that way will suffice in forming a workable idea of the market, providing all account managers structurally and conscientiously record this kind of data the whole year round.

Again, it is key here that apples be compared to apples. Discount scales lower per-unit net prices as customers purchase greater volumes. The diagram below depicts pricing structures whereby price is offset against volume.

This approach provides insight into variations in prices of a particular piece of software at three suppliers (see Figure 15).

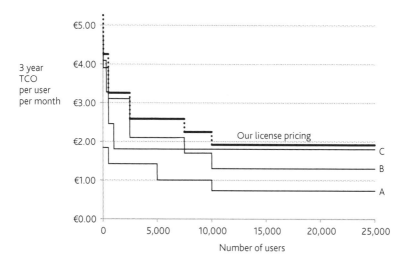

Figure 15 Analysis of competitor prices (3-year TCO) for corporate software (fictitious data)

We can see that supplier C is fairly competitive in the market when the software is used by up to 5,000 users. Only supplier A's price is lower. Above 5,000 users, C's price is less attractive. The distance to supplier A grows as soon as the number of users exceeds 5,000. Above 8,000 users, supplier B's price is also lower than that of supplier C.

We have turned this comparison into a like-with-like comparison in two ways, using a process that is referred to as *normalization*. First, we included the number of users in the comparison by offsetting the price per user against the total volume, instead of only considering one single figure. And secondly we made a correction for different price parameters. Two popular revenue models for software are the licensing model and the subscription model. These two models do not lend themselves to one-to-one comparison.

The licensing model charges customers a one-off amount for software ownership (the license) and a separate fee for maintenance and support. In the case of the subscription model, customers subscribe to the software, maintenance, and support for a monthly fee.

The normalization measure we introduced was to spread total cost of ownership (TCO) out over three years. This TCO is made up of licensing, maintenance, and support costs for three years of use. Thanks to this normalization, pricing models can be compared with the greatest possible accuracy.*

2. Customized offers

A tailored offer will only specify the total net price. In this case, a salesperson will not deliver a price or discount list along with the offer. This kind of customization can be taken to an extreme where every customer receives a different price proposal. Customized offers therefore obscure price visibility. An offer only relates to the individual needs of an individual customer. However, customers often show (parts of) offers by competitors to all potential suppliers to be able to better weigh up their options. Sales staff will then point out the weaker points and conditions of competitors and further explain the points that the customer considers to be weak points of their own proposal.

When normalizing the offers by other suppliers, we can, however, still use information from customized offers to offset our prices against. For the example of corporate software, we have analyzed a few normalized observations of individual offers in the same diagram as we used for the price lists. The vertical axis represents the per-unit price, while the horizontal axis shows the volume.

Subsequently, we will combine the information extracted from price lists to that from the offers (see Figure 16). Our example contains three additional observations of customized offers. Prices are €3.44, €0.80, and €1.44 at user volumes of 2,000, 7,000, and 22,000 respectively. This paints a more complete picture, because we have more information to go by.

---

* The choice for a period of three years is somewhat arbitrary. A longer period would make the licensing model cheaper, while a shorter period would tip the scales in favor of the subscription model.

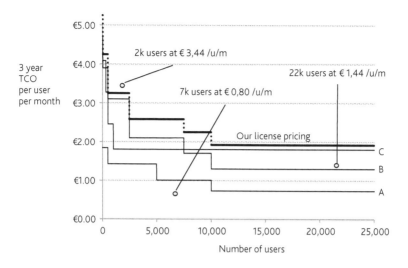

Figure 16 Market price analysis of corporate software based on price lists and offers (fictitious data)

3. Win/loss data

Even without any knowledge of competitors' prices, you can get an idea of the market price. You can track the trends in your own sales processes. This information is then used to plot volume and average per-unit price against each other on two axes, both for offers that were successful and those that were not.

The chart depicts the correlation between offer price and the success of the sales process. This connection provides an estimate of the market price. If a clear connection is lacking, this can be down to several causes. The number of observations may be insufficient, for example, or the required normalization has not yet been performed. Shipping costs per kilogram are, for example, difficult to compare without a correction for distance or journey time. A third reason might be that price has little influence on whether an offer is successful or not.

Example

A company provides promotional services to manufacturers of consumer goods. To make its prices more consistent, it has decided to revamp its price list (see Figure 17).

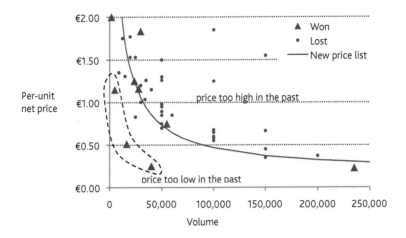

Figure 17 Example of a win/loss analysis. Prices varied greatly in the past. The new price list introduces structure and is in line with market conditions (fictitious data)

The company uses win/loss data to recalibrate the level of its prices and discounts.

The new pricing structure follows the boundary between win and loss (see Figure 17). Net prices approximate the market ratio of price to value (C3 and C4). This will boost chances of offers being successful, while keeping discounts as low as possible.

4. Research firms

Research firms are another source of data on prices of competitors. These are specialist parties that collect market data in various markets. Providers such as AC Nielsen and GfK sell descriptive data about prices and volumes for many consumer products.

Even when data is not directly related to price, you can sometimes still extract indirect prices or price levels. A research firm will, for example, provide information regarding revenues and volumes of manufacturers per type of machine. Dividing revenue by volume will give you the average price for a machine segment. This price in itself is not very accurate, but charting the development of average prices over the years will point at price fluctuations in the market.

10.2.3 VALUE OF THE PROPOSITION

Extrapolating an indication of the value of the proposition (C3) is harder than deducing implicit information about prices or separate elements of the proposition. That is because the former requires an idea of all value drivers and prices. And on top of that, it requires understanding of the interplay that determines customer value.

Value drivers

One possible approach can be to go over all available information about propositions and value drivers in the market. This would involve using our expert judgment to estimate the importance of each value driver for the customer. We can deduce price-to-value ratios from that assessment. Section 5.2 (Customer Value) outlines this procedure in its description of the price drivers of value and competition (C3 en C4), and includes an example that illustrates the price-to-value ratio of mid-range cars.

Chain analysis

Another way of assessing the value of your proposition is by conducting a chain analysis, i.e., to gauge the savings and value customers, and customers' customers, get when using your product or service. For example: a waste-processing company that helps a customer reduce the amount of waste it produces, hence increasing its customer's efficiency. This way, the waste-processing company provides more value than competitors who merely pick up tons of waste, without making suggestions for production chain improvements. Another example would be the selection of materials for aircraft manufacturing. One parts supplier offers value added through stronger and lighter wings. Thanks to these parts, the aircraft manufacturer can raise its prices because it is offering its customers better fuel economy.

Example: food quality improvement

A supplier of ingredients boasts a patented technique that helps it prevent bacterial contamination of food. Its solution reduces the chance of contamination for the food industry.

Reduction of contaminated food

A chain analysis is a suitable way of evaluating the value of this technique, which helps the food maker reduce the amount of contaminated food it produces. Since this food will have to be destroyed, all costs of production are considered a loss. The value of this loss is calculated from the quantity of contaminated food valued at "ex-factory" prices.

We distinguish three further value components for the manufacturer. These are: higher brand value, lower risk on claims, and prevention of production interruptions.

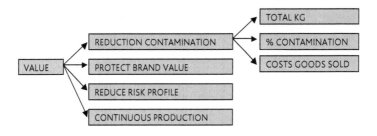

Figure 18 Value analysis for prevention of food contamination

Brand value

Food contaminated by dangerous bacteria can cause death or serious illness among the population. Besides the human drama, there is also great potential reputational risk for the manufacturer's brand value. The supplier's patented solution lowers this risk and therefore protects brand value.

Risk profile

The newly developed product greatly reduces the risk of consumers filing claims due to food contamination. Moreover, in a possible court case, the food manufacturer can now rely on the argument that he uses state-of-the-art technology.

Continuous production

The prevention of production downtime represents value added for the manufacturer. That is because every case of contamination involves the destruction of an entire batch and temporary shutting down of the production process. Only when problems have been completely sorted out can the manufacturer restart the production line, while it will also be a while before production speed is back to optimum levels.

Based on an estimate of the financial value of these four components, you can define the price as a part of the delivered total value.

In this case, the sales process is based on value based selling.[64] Sales professionals will highlight savings and their value for the potential customer in a business case presented during sales pitches. The supplier reports realization of the forecast savings for the food manufacturer during the usage of the product. This fact-based sales approach will persuade all stakeholders at the manufacturer's organization, which are also referred to as buying influences.* The switch to the new solution is broadly supported across the company.[65] Implementation is completed quickly and successfully.

10.3   Demand side

On the demand side, customers determine the success of the price proposition. Their response to a price change depends on their needs, means (budget), and perceptions. This applies both in B2B markets and in retail or B2C environments. This section will deal with the indicators of price sensitivity.

10.3.1   CONSUMER MARKETS

Consumers have varying levels of willingness to pay for services or products. Their appraisal of a proposition can be extrapolated from:
- personal preference and need
- budgetary means
- share of wallet
- buying behavior
- perception

---

* Buying influences are various roles that influence a company's decision-making on a purchase. Important roles are: user, economic buyer, and technical buyer

The influence of *personal preference and need* is obvious. When someone's tastes or needs change, this will influence their willingness to pay. On the other hand, unknown is unloved, i.e., not willing to pay. When launching new products, marketing's overriding aim is therefore to get people to try to it out. That is more important than the price at that stage. Price promotions and trial periods are a popular way of tempting consumers to try out a product or service.

Budgetary means determine responses to price changes. This should be seen in relation to the *relative costs* of the purchase. These relative costs are measured as the share of wallet. The greater the share of wallet represented by a product, the greater the impact of a change to the price of that product.

Consumers' *buying behavior* gives an indication of price sensitivity. Behavior patterns are a source of information throughout the entire purchasing process, from initial orientation up to post-purchase satisfaction. In the case of supermarkets, a key indicator is how customers respond when their favorite brand is not available. The more customers decide to go for another brand, the more price sensitive the brand is. Tracking this kind of data is part of the activities of market research firms.

Perceptions play a major role, as we saw in Chapter 6 (C7). Perception differs per cost item. Many people will change supermarket to save five euros a week, but not insurer to save twenty euros a month. Perception also has an effect inside one and the same shop. Supermarkets use keenly priced C brands to seem cheaper overall. They know customers mainly go for medium-range B brands out of an urge to reduce uncertainty (refer to Section 6.2.4).

Few companies succeed in utilizing all available data about customers and their behavior. As part of a structured approach, you will first have to chart all indicative variables for the target group. After measuring the indicators and drawing up clear reports, pricing intelligence is rolled out in the business to support the pricing policy based on data. You can gather this data yourself from customer information or other IT systems. Market research departments at major corporations have a huge wealth of information from which they can draw and which was initially collected for purposes other than pricing.

Table 8 is an example of indicators in the FMCG industry.[*] Companies operating in this sector will normally have the required data ready to hand, because they already use it for marketing purposes. Many consumer goods manufacturers have a large product portfolio, making it hard for managers to get a clear idea of which products could do with a better price. The overview of indicators highlights prices that need closer scrutiny.

Customer characteristics	Rise ↑ coincides with:
■ Unique preferences (mass vs. niche) ■ Customer's budget ■ Loyalty (product/brand/category) ■ Time spent in front of shelf when choosing ■ % postponement of purchase when "regular product/brand/ category not available" ■ % planned purchase ahead of shop visit	Price sensitivity ↓ Price ↑
■ How well do customers know products, brands, category, and shops? ■ How well do customers know the prices?	Price sensitivity ↑ Price ↓
Propositions (value drivers)	**Rise ↑ coincides with:**
■ Promotion (type of media/budget/effectiveness) ■ Place (quality of channels/retailers/outlets) ■ Product (quality, options, brand image)	Price sensitivity ↓ Price ↑
■ Strength of competition's marketing mix	Price sensitivity ↑ Price ↓

Table 8 Price sensitivity indicators for FMCG

For example, customers can be considered loyal to a product when the percentage of planned purchases or the percentage of postponed purchases is high. In that case, a higher price seems possible. The fact-based approach uses all indicators from Table 8 to identify products with a price which is potentially too high or too low.[†] Effects of price changes can be gauged afterwards.

---

[*] FMCG: fast-moving consumer goods
[†] The customer characteristics in Table 8 are related to the demand side, the propositions (value drivers) relate to the supply side (see Section 10.2)

10.4   Market outcomes

In the previous paragraphs, we dealt with indications of price sensitivity on the supply side by comparing propositions and prices. This was followed by a review of the demand side, for which we focused on customer behavior.

The final section of this chapter will now look at information about results in the market. Whenever supply meets demand, transactions ensue. Information about sales volume and market shares provides useful indications of price sensitivity.

10.4.1   EXAMPLE: MARKET SHARE AND PRICE CHANGE

In 2003, Dutch market leader Albert Heijn overhauled its pricing policy. Its new policy presented the company as a supermarket with a superior (broad) assortment and medium-level prices instead of its traditional proposition of medium to high-end products at high prices. The company used marketing communication and selective price cuts to get this new image across. Simultaneously to Albert Heijn's revamp, the market as a whole also saw several major changes. The Jumbo supermarket chain grew from a regional player to the national number 2 in 2012. Jumbo is a service-driven chain with a broad range of products with a "lowest price guarantee". And to top it all off, a competitor at the higher end of the market, Laurus, was driven to bankruptcy by poor management and price constraints.

Albert Heijn's market share grew significantly after the introduction of its new pricing policy. This is a solid indication that lower prices did indeed make Albert Heijn more attractive, which resulted in more sales. This is, however, not conclusive proof. Albert Heijn's market share growth could, after all, also be down to improvements in its assortment, its better marketing communication, or its competitor Laurus going into administration. Market share therefore constitutes an implicit, and not an explicit, measurement of the effect of price changes.

There are many indicators, also known as key performance indicators (KPI), for results in the market. Popular KPIs are margin, revenue, sales volume, market share, and market size. The advantage of sales volume, revenue, and margin is that these can be measured using internal data, which is often readily available. Choosing an unsuitable KPI, however, has serious consequences. Although hitting a challenging sales target may bring the desired market share in terms of volume, accompanying cost increases may very well eat up the margin.

10.4.2 EXAMPLE: SLOW AND FAST MOVERS

The fashion industry is subject to the whims of consumers. Since fashion items are often only produced for one season, it is always nerve-racking to see whether purchased stock flies off the racks or is snubbed by consumers. Unsold items will go for less in the end-of-season sales. That is when customers are already looking forward to the new collection, and expect a discount on leftovers from last season. Keeping these left-over items in stock is furthermore expensive. But when a certain item is completely sold out halfway through the season, the price turned out to be too low. What's more, a higher price would have had an anchoring effect on the prices of other items (C7).

Some fashion retailers use sales data therefore as an indicator for possible price changes. A few weeks into the season, slow movers become eligible for a price cut. Fast movers are eligible for a price rise. A retailer may even consider ordering another batch of the item in question from the manufacturer to replenish stock. This tactic brings price interventions forward, instead of waiting until the sales at the end of the season.

The analysis of sales velocity departs from the "apples to apples" principle. Comparing sales of a dress to sales of a pair of pants is not a meaningful exercise, simply because the product groups of dresses and pants have different sales rhythms throughout the season. Sales velocity comparisons are therefore restricted to one product group.

It should be noted here that sales will be hampered by having a smaller size range in stock. This will force shop staff to disappoint customers more often. It is for that reason that we do not only measure sales velocity as *sales volume*, but also as *sales from stock*, which is sales volume divided by stock position.

We have plotted these indicators against each other on two axes for one product group (see Figure 19). Slow movers are those items for which sales volume and sales from stock are low. For fast movers, on the other hand, these two indicators show a high value.

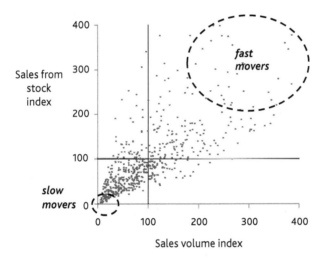

Figure 19 Identification of slow and fast movers in fashion retail (indexed). Index = 100 represents the average of all items (fictitious data)

Slow movers qualify for a mark-down, while fast movers should be considered for a mark-up. To help him make the actual decision about the price of these products, the category manager or pricing manager will receive a report with a brief outline of the situation of each item (see Figure 20).

This report briefs the decision-maker on sales volume and stock position over the three most recent weeks (week numbers 15, 16, and 17). Relative sales velocity (fast, slow, or neither) is derived from that information. In order to facilitate interpretation of these results, price changes from those same weeks, as well as any discounts given

Product	Color	Sales			Stock			Fast or slow			Price change			Discount%			Price	Price
		15	16	17	15	16	17	15	16	17	15	16	17	15	16	17	START	17
79117	brown	2	1	0	508	507	507							0%	0%	0%	€160	€160
	gray	3	2	1	432	430	429							0%	0%	0%	€160	€160
	blue	2	1	0	325	324	324							0%	0%	0%	€160	€160
79118	beige	9	2	4	258	256	252							0%	0%	0%	€130	€130
	gray	10	10	3	213	203	200							-2%	0%	0%	€130	€130
79120	white	32	17	9	582	565	556							1%	0%	0%	€140	€140
	pink	10	0	1	663	663	662							0%	0%	0%	€140	€140
79227	beige	31	10	4	958	948	944				-€25		€27	0%	0%	5%	€140	€100
	gray	38	17	1	982	965	964				-€25		€27	1%	1%	-9%	€140	€101
	white	31	26	5	263	237	232				-€25		€27	0%	0%	-7%	€140	€100
	red	14	10	0	643	633	633				-€25			0%	0%	0%	€140	€100

Figure 20 Report on fast and slow movers (fictitious data)

through in-store promotions, are listed as well. The last two columns list the original price at the start of the season and the current price in week 17. This ensures efficient and meaningful use of the available commercial data to enable sound decision-making about price changes.

A few weeks further down the line, the pricing manager or the category manager will be able to evaluate the effects price changes had on sales volume in a second performance report. In Chapter 11 we will discuss methods that can be used to do that.

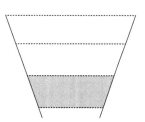

CHAPTER 11

Explicit measurement (layer 3)

11.1 Introduction

The third layer of the pricing funnel consists of explicit measurement of the effects of price changes. The objective here is to obtain a full and accurate understanding of the influence of price. The approach of this layer has more solid scientific underpinning and can be costly.[66] Explicit measurement does not necessarily provide the best results at every company. The required attention to detail and the laborious nature of working with technical and mathematical models may obscure the view of the bigger picture. The pricing strategy and revenue model will subsequently suffer the consequences of that.

Application of the methods explained in the following makes most sense when precision is paramount. The more accessible information from layers 1 and 2 must not be neglected. Layers 1 and 2 are more quickly available and applicable, but also serve to assess the correct set-up, method, and technical execution of explicit measurements. The ambition of the third layer is to understand complex connections between multiple variables that define the price. And this ambition is both the strength and weakness of the methods from this layer.

Take a company that, for example, has realized significant cost savings. It has seen its net profit rise slightly thanks to lower costs and growth in its market share resulting from lower selling price levels. Boards will generally be very content with that kind of result, and have little need for a complex mathematical analysis of the correlations between costs, price, competition, consumer demand, and profit.

Besides accuracy, explicit measurement offers another benefit. Making models creates better-quality understanding of the system of interrelations between provider, customer, costs, value, competitors, partners, suppliers, and so on. These qualitative insights can engender new perspectives on strategy, business model, and revenue model. And they will also improve utilization and interpretation of the first and second layer of the pricing funnel.

This chapter will go into three kinds of explicit measurement methods. The division between these three is based on the source of the data they use:
- Buying behavior
- Experiments
- Preferences

11.2 Buying behavior

11.2.1 REALITY AS THE STARTING POINT

In this section, we will discuss models of buying behavior that assess price sensitivity based on *actual* choices by customers. In compiling these models, customers were observed during transactions or details of transactions were recorded. Seeing as information about the behavior of customers is always based on the past, these models do not lend themselves very well to extrapolation of the effects of new products or new pricing models.

Many companies have the kind of detailed data available to them that application of these models require. When selling online, collecting that information is fairly straightforward, as you can piece together customers' buying patterns on the website. In a B2B setting, direct contacts with customers provide an opportunity to track the buying process using sophisticated CRM* systems. Offline retailers have a wealth of information about buying behavior in their POS systems.† And they also gather additional data through loyalty cards and in-store data collectors, such as a footfall counter. The trick is to set up data processes and IT systems in a way that ensures adequate ordering of observations and logical definition of the data structure. Only then will they help produce meaningful pricing analyses.

There are, however, also companies that lack access to observations. Suppliers who work through indirect channels often do not have any information about transactions of end consumers. They often resort to hiring external research firms to gather data through customer surveys. This data is then unrelated to the actual buying process.

11.2.2 ECONOMETRIC MODELS

Compiling a statistical model that is intended to measure price elasticity takes us into the realm of econometrics. This is a discipline that uses sophisticated models to assess the most likely relationship between economic variables.[67] Econometrics starts with an *assumed* relationship, such as a correlation between sales volume, market share, and price. This assumption will be based on economic theory or a brilliant idea by a pricing strategist. The second step is to measure the variables in reality. The quality of the estimation of the relationship is largely dependent on the quality of the data collected. Here too, the adage "garbage in = garbage out" applies.

The data and the theoretic link are the point of departure for statistical tests. An econometrist will finally arrive at a conclusion about the most probable relationship between variables such as market share, price, and sales volume. His conclusion will not be infallible. A test of the "significance" of the influence of price results is an indication

---

* CRM: Customer Relationship Management. This is software for management and commercial use of all customer information with features such as customer name details, order status, …, but also offers and prices
† POS: Point of Sale

of the level of *probability* of price affecting, for example, the sales volume. These tests do, however, not address alternative models.

An econometrist will use the assumed relationship to make predictions. He will estimate price sensitivity and determine which explanatory factors are more probable. Statements on probability are only valid when the model was specified correctly in the first place. Franses and Paap showed how complicated it is to specify a model that adheres to reality. Their study makes an estimation of weekly Heinz tomato ketchup sales at varying prices and with different promotions using AC Nielsen data. This data was collected at a supermarket in South Dakota between 1985 and 1988.[68] Obvious models did not always turn out to be up to the job.[*]

Franses and Paap compared model structures and definitions of variables. There are many different ways of quantifying commercial issues. In a model that specifies purchases, for example, we will find various ways of defining variables. The research can focus on the observation of "sale or no sale", or the specific brand that was chosen. Another alternative is to perform analyses on a higher level and attempt to explain the sum of purchases. Individual purchases will then no longer be an explicit part of the model. The explanatory variables used also contain a specification choice. You can, for example, use the current price or last week's price. The latter may perhaps play a role in the consumer's perception.

Market researchers, pricing analysts, and software vendors are not always aware of the pitfalls Franses and Paap describe. And at the same time, executives and pricing managers struggle with the interpretation of statistical data. Many of the models are like a black box to them. Decision-makers prefer simple transparent guidelines that are aligned with their experience. And they want to be able to share results of analyses in their teams and across the organization. It may therefore be productive to use simple models, with specifications that are in sync with perception, instead of endless statistical tests.

---

[*] Franses and Paap have analyzed the pitfalls of models that are widely used by econometrists and market researchers (OLS, logit, multinomial logit, ...).

These simple models will also better dovetail with the less detailed information produced by the first two FPF layers.

In the remainder of this section we will present examples of simple models from layer 3 that are suited to implementation across a broader team. Reducing the number of additional variables to one intuitively logical factor will maximize comprehensibility of the outcome of these models. The downside to these methods is that their statistical explanatory force is inferior to that of more thought-out and complex models.

11.2.3 LIMITATION TO ONE ADDITIONAL VARIABLE

In many cases, one single variable can capture a wide range of influences. If this variable also resonates with people in the workplace, a model can provide an informative and transparent idea of the relationship. A complex analysis of all factors will only be informative once, and only to a specialist. For day-to-day pricing decisions, simplicity outweighs accuracy.

11.2.4 EXAMPLE: AIRLINE INDUSTRY

In the airline industry, price and quality of a route are important buying factors. The quality of a route is determined by multiple aspects, such as the number of flights, travel time, punctuality, departure and arrival times, and available capacity. It is quite conceivable to compose a complex statistical model that calculates a fair share for each route. The fair share is the market share the model expects for the offered route. This fair share is an indicator of the quality of the route.

A relatively simple pricing system will subsequently offset this fair share against the actual market share. The idea behind that is to check whether the price level is too high or too low, and whether it is in line with strategic guidelines for markets and routes. If the market share exceeds the fair share, pricing may be aggressive. But if the market share stays below the fair share, a price cut could be called for.

11.2.5 EXAMPLE: FASHION

Quick evaluation of price performance is of major importance to fashion retailers. Restricted to seasons, fashion retailers can only use the instrument of price changes over a short period of time. Identification of slow and fast movers will yield opportunities for price rises and cuts (refer to 10.4.2). Category managers subsequently require a review of each price change to assess whether or not it was successful.

This analysis, however, is a complex one. Numerous factors can influence sales volume, such as fashion trends, seasons, weather, economic climate, store staff quality, competitive landscape, quality of retailer's store and collection, stocking levels, quality and prices of alternative items from retailer's collection, etc. Consequently, coming up with an econometric model is certainly not a walk in the park. And there is also a considerable chance that the model's specifications are unstable. After all, the model can change every month: the role of the factor season can change from one year to the next, or a variable left out one month may turn out to be significant after all the next month, forcing the econometrist to recalibrate the models.

In practice, model specifications are often not reassessed. Companies use results produced by models specified a long time ago. We will now deal with the alternative of a simplified model. We will look at the price and sales volume of an item and the average price and sales volume of the corresponding product group. We will not include any other explanatory variables. The average sales volume for the product group represents the influence of all factors we have not included. Higher revenue generated by an item after a price rise is not necessarily a good sign: when average revenue for the product group goes up at a faster rate, the item in question will in a relative sense be considered to be underperforming.

Table 9 shows data for the evaluation of a price rise for a winter coat. Sales volume for the item dropped 6.5% due to the price rise. In order to introduce a correction that allows us to consider external developments, we will look at the relative drop in volume in comparison to the sales volume for the overall product group. This corrected drop is less, namely 3%.

Nevertheless, the price rise turns out well. The higher price outweighs the lower volume. Revenue and margin of the coat were up 9.1% and 21.1% respectively. And when we introduce the same product group correction as above, these increases even go up to 11.1% and 21.9%.

Item 120339, Wool winter coat – point design

Product group: Long winter coats. Purchase price: €43,78. VAT: 19%

			Price change evaluation	
Item	Before	After	Direct	Relative
Price	€119,95	€139,95	16,7%	14,5%
Sales (units)	185	173	−6,5%	−3,0%
Revenue	€18.648	€20.346	9,1%	11,1%
Margin	€10.548	€12.772	21,1%	21,9%

Product group	Before	After		
Price (average)	€132,85	€135,34	1,9%	
Sales (units)	7.215	6.954	−3,6%	
Revenue	€805.473	€790.886	−1,8%	
Margin	€489.600	€486.440	−0,6%	

Table 9 Evaluation of a price change for a winter coat (fictitious data)

Figures concerning the *direct* change in sales volume, revenue, and margin are recognizable and instantly understandable. The correction for the product group shows the relative change when factoring in circumstances such as fashion trends, weather, in-store promotions, and so on. Category managers consider it a logical move to view changes in light of those seen in the overall product group. They will then sooner trust the outcome and it also makes implementation quicker and more complete.

11.2.6 COMPARATIVE DATA

Deal makers make little structural use of historic data in contract negotiations. They will brush analyses based on two hundred offers with a similar scope aside and go by their own experience with five or ten offers, each with a different scope. Model-based insights extracted from previous transactions that form a black box therefore have less impact than they could have. A solution to this could be to give deal makers access to the data itself. To give them the opportunity to benchmark base figures such as price, volume, service level, etc. in their pitch against offers from the past.

11.2.7   EXAMPLE: MANAGED DOCUMENT SERVICES

A major bank sends a document services provider a request for proposal (RFP[*]) for a managed service, specifying requirements for maintenance, help desk support, service level management, general support, and paper and ink replenishment. The client requires efficient machinery with the main prerequisites being the number of units per FTE and print speed.

In preparing the proposal for the potential client, the account manager at the document services provider discusses the "win price" with the pricing manager, i.e., the price that will land them the contract. The pricing manager delves into the European historic database and digs out all previously submitted tenders to major banks (see Table 10a). He goes by data from across Europe because three of the four competitors are coordinating a deal of these proportions on a European scale.

The price level in the market is subsequently estimated based on the overview of previous tender processes. The analysis exclusively looks at tenders for managed services at major financial institutions. More complex econometric models explaining the influence of the type of service and the client's industry are not required. There is, however, one downside to this practical approach in that it fails to make the most of information about other industries or types of service.

---

[*]   RFP: request for proposal. An RFP is a document in which a client specifies all his requirements to potential suppliers. As part of an RFP process, the client will send the RFP to one or multiple providers, expecting a comprehensive proposal back within a specific time frame, following which they will decide which provider they will award the contract, possibly after further negotiations.

| | | This prospect | A | B | C | D | E | F < past prospects |
		RFP	Won	Lost	Won	Won	Lost	Lost < outcomes
Hardware price	/unit	TBD	€4,789	€4,320	€7,144	€5,194	€4,580	€3,909
Service fee forecast	million		€7.8	€4.2	€13.9	€2.6	€11.8	€20.8
Service fee	B/W	TBD	0.0118	0.0110	0.0110	0.0130	0.0120	0.0105
(€/copy)	Color	TBD	0.0950	0.0950	0.0880	0.1050	0.0975	0.0950
Units	#	775	689	375	1200	273	1060	1149
Copiers	B/W	77	69	37	120	82	106	115
	Color	466	345	245	840	82	636	575
Printers	B/W	116	172	18	60	82	159	287
	Color	116	103	75	180	27	159	172
Speed	Copier	39	40	29	49	34	34	29
(pag/min)	Printer	29	25	24	39	24	19	24
Term	months	60	48	60	60	48	60	72
Volume	B/W	64.8	55.1	28.3	73.6	24.0	81.1	101.1
(mio/yr)	Color	20.5	13.8	5.5	22.4	3.3	14.3	25.3
% print		5%	3%	1%	3%	3%	2%	3%

Table 10a Tender data for managed photocopying services *before normalization* (fictitious data).

The pricing manager will now normalize six offers from previous tender processes for the hardware and service scope (Table 10b). This normalization mainly concerns speed, percentage, color copies, number of units, and number of printouts. Having normalized these figures, the pricing manager discusses bid tactics and account strategy with sales management. Together, they decide on a price of €5,400 per unit for the hardware, €0.011 per black-and-white printout, and €0.090 per color printout. The pricing manager then goes on to draw up the business case using the standard template and submits it to the board.

| | | This prospect | A | B | C | D | E | F < past prospects |
		RFP	Won	Lost	Won	Won	Lost	Lost < outcomes
TCO (millions)		€17.0	€11.1	€5.8	€22.5	€4.0	€16.7	€25.3
Normalized hardware costs		€4.2	€3.6	€4.5	€4.4	€4.6	€4.1	€4.1
Normalized service fee		€12.8	€10.8	€13.3	€12.6	€12.0	€13.9	€15.7
Normalized TCO		€17.0	€14.5	€17.8	€17.0	€16.6	€17.9	€19.8
Result		RFP	Won	Lost	Won	Won	Lost	Lost
Hardware price	/unit	€5,400	€4,789	€4,320	€7,144	€5,194	€4,580	€3,909
Service fee forecast	million		€7.8	€4.2	€13.9	€2.6	€11.8	€20.8
Service fee	B/W	0.0110	0.0118	0.0110	0.0110	0.0130	0.0120	0.0105
(€/copy)	Color	0.0900	0.0950	0.0950	0.0880	0.1050	0.0975	0.0950

Table 10b TCO win price analysis *after normalization* (fictitious data).

11.3 Experiments

Price experiments have one clear advantage over the methods from the previous section (11.2): they enable research into prices of propositions that have not yet been officially launched in the market, but which are fully developed. Where behavior-based analyses go by past prices and transactions, experiments allow for assessment of new pricing models and products.

An adequate test requires a controlled sales environment and a sufficient number of observations. Retail chains effortlessly set up experiments at pilot stores, where they charge prices that differ from those at their regular stores. E-commerce websites selectively offer customers an alternative webpage with test prices and record responses. The difference in sales volume before and after the price change at the test store suggests certain price sensitivity levels. Needless to say, sales achieved at regular stores are equally susceptible to external influences during the test period, such as the fashion season, holidays, the weather, and so on. Regular stores therefore serve as the control group for effects identified at test stores. When the weather is bad for a week, this will be visibly reflected in the sales at regular stores. That would then be an effect that was not triggered by the test price.

Working experiments out into models presents a statistical challenge. Full discretion in designing the set-up provides control over the experiment, but a model must describe external influences to be able to make corrections wherever necessary. Including a large number of variables may increase explanatory force, but it will also complicate interpretation.

11.4 Preferences

11.4.1 RESPONDENTS

Whenever a controlled sales environment is not feasible, measuring preferences makes for a good alternative to experiments. Companies with indirect sales channels will often resort to this, bringing in market research firms to perform such measurements. These researchers will question respondents in an isolated setting. There are direct and indirect methods for doing so.[69] Direct methods ask questions that are directly related to price sensitivity, while indirect methods also cover other elements in their questioning.

The upside of this approach is that the method can also be applied for products and services that have not yet been (fully) developed. Aside from pricing managers, customer preferences are also of interest to product managers, business development managers, and R&D managers. Preference measurement provides them with the information they need to define optimum specifications of possible propositions.

The downside of gauging preferences is that respondents reply what they *would* do if they *were in a position where they would have to* choose from the presented alternatives. The option of not buying anything is difficult to study, because respondents are not considering an actual purchase. Conclusions will not be based on actual behavior, while conclusions emerging from analysis of buying behavior (11.2) and experiments (11.3) are. Behavioral research has shown that people are not always aware of the choices they actually make.[*] Measuring preferences will therefore not necessarily produce workable information.

11.4.2 DIRECT MEASUREMENT

A direct measurement asks respondents which price they consider reasonable. There are several ways[†] of gauging their perception of price reasonableness using multiple questions such as:

- "At which price would you consider this product to be cheap?"
- "At which price would you consider this product so cheap that it would cause you to start doubting its quality?"
- "Would you buy this product for €10?"

---

* Also refer to Chapter 6
† Examples include the "Van Westendorp" and the "Gabor Granger" methods.

The questions are simple. The answers are less reliable, as people are often unable to truthfully answer these kinds of direct questions. They need a context to be able to judge prices.[*]

11.4.3 INDIRECT MEASUREMENT

In the case of indirect preference measurement,[†] a researcher will present respondents with multiple choices. These choices cover several features of the proposition, including the price. Respondents will be asked to state which alternative they prefer. And they will do so several times in a row for different questions. Figure 21 is an example of the choice of an airline ticket from a study into the value of extras such as a drink or in-flight entertainment.

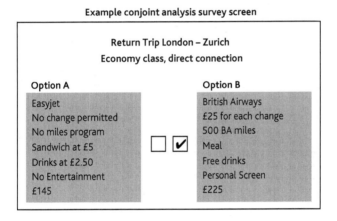

Example conjoint analysis survey screen

Return Trip London – Zurich

Economy class, direct connection

Option A

Easyjet
No change permitted
No miles program
Sandwich at £5
Drinks at £2.50
No Entertainment
£145

Option B

British Airways
£25 for each change
500 BA miles
Meal
Free drinks
Personal Screen
£225

Figure 21 Sample question screen for indirect preference measurement for flights (fictitious data)

The choices respondents make are used to estimate price sensitivity for each feature. By equating the respondents as a group to the market, you can deduce market shares at different prices and with differing product features. Seeing as you will ask the same questions for competitors' products, you will also be mapping competitiveness and market dynamics.

---

[*] Also refer to Chapter 6
[†] Examples include "discrete choice analysis" and "conjoint analysis"

PART III

The execution of pricing

CHAPTER 12

Challenge

12.1 Opportunities

Implementing a revenue model and optimizing prices using fact-based methods is by no means a casual affair. It is something that affects all parts of the company. The challenge of the execution of pricing is the subject of this third part of the book.

The way in which pricing and price strategy are organized does generally not stand out for its transparency. Even though pricing is a primary business process, it is not as well organized as other business processes.[*] That is a huge missed opportunity, as there is great potential for improvement in the execution of pricing. In 2006, General Electric CEO Jeffrey Immelt spoke the following words:

> "Not long ago, a guy here ... did an analysis of our pricing in appliances and found out that about $5 billion of it is discretionary. ... It was the most astounding number I'd ever heard — and that's just in appliances.

---

[*] Also refer to Chapter 2

Extrapolating across our businesses, there may be $50 billion that few people are tracking or accountable for. We would never allow something like that on the cost side. ... But with the prices we charge, we're too sloppy."[70]

A 2011 study showed that of all Fortune 500 companies in the US, under 5% have an expert on their staff who focuses exclusively on pricing, and earlier findings indicate that only a small minority conduct systematic price research.[71]

Today, in the year 2013, pricing is rapidly moving up corporate agendas. This chapter will briefly explain what kinds of problems you may come up against in your attempts to take the execution of pricing to a higher level. We will provide backgrounds to the design of pricing processes and describe the organization of the pricing function. After we have explored the playing field in this chapter, Chapters 13, 14, 15, and 16 will set out the features of an optimum pricing process and optimum pricing function.

12.2 Nature of the process

Over the past few decades, companies have extensively defined and documented primary processes relating to sales, production, and financial administration. BPR projects have drawn on methods such as six sigma and total quality management to optimize these processes using information technology. Performance measurement has become part of everyday business. KPIs provide management with direction. Pricing processes, on the other hand, do not receive the same treatment, which is odd, considering the importance of price. This is partly down to the fact that pricing responsibilities are not clearly allocated. There is no obvious leader who takes the bull by the horns.

Another reason underlying the lack of attention for the pricing process may be the nature of the output. The output, a "price", is an abstract intangible figure. Other business processes do produce concrete output: sales produces "orders", and production churns out "products". Orders and products are more engaging than the numbers that make up prices. A price is easier to reproduce than the output of many other processes. When a customer orders a sofa, the furniture store cannot sell this customer a sofa that has already been bought by another customer. A sofa is a unique *physical* product. You cannot sell the same product twice. A price, however, can be reproduced numerous times. There is nothing as easy as using one and the same price for all customers and retail instances. By keeping prices steady throughout the year or simply inflation indexing your prices when there is no acute reason to change a price you will save yourself a lot of hassle.

12.3 Second invisible hand

Responsibilities, skills, and information about pricing are widespread at many companies. An explicit, clear, and broadly supported pricing strategy, however, is often lacking. Price sensitivity measurement is not a structural part of commercial activities. That is partly why pricing is a kind of Pandora's Box for the board of many a company. Managers and policy-makers are reluctant to open it. Their (subconscious) fear is that making the pricing process explicit will trigger too many questions from too many different sides. Organization and coordination of pricing hence remain implicit and insufficiently defined. Everybody has an opinion about the price, but no one is responsible. This shortcoming is what we call the "second invisible hand of pricing".[72]

12.4 Balance

Armed with the knowledge of the art and the science of pricing from previous chapters, this part of the book will answer questions that arise in the (re)organization of pricing:
- "Who will be in charge of pricing?"
- "Where should pricing go in the organizational set-up?"
- "How will pricing work together with other primary business functions?"
- "What is the right change approach toward a mature pricing capability?"

Pricing requires specific competencies and targeted intelligence. Final decisions in this area are made by the executive who is responsible for profits, often the CEO of the relevant business unit or the company. Information for that decision comes from all sections of the company and its environment. The analysis (science) and creativity (art) that are needed are difficult to reconcile with the day-to-day concerns of top-level management (CEO, CFO, COO, CCO).[*]

Balance between specializing in pricing tasks and integrating[73] pricing into other business processes is an essential prerequisite when setting up the pricing function. Specialization is needed to improve the quality of execution on the level of details. Integration is required to enable strategic consideration and to garner support from functions such as marketing, sales, and finance. The business owner needs an integrated perspective on price. The job of setting prices was therefore the exclusive territory of this particular executive. After all, his or her coordinating position gave him or her access to the best and most comprehensive information. Over the past few decades, however, IT technology has made it possible for pricing specialists to manage and integrate all that information. They support or even partly take on the decision-making.

12.5 Development

Optimum organizational structuring and high-quality pricing mutually reinforce each other. Improvements to the pricing policy and ensuing business successes necessitate changes in the heart of the organization. Better organization of the pricing function will subsequently lead to better prices and results. This interplay enables a natural and gradual development path toward the best possible pricing function. Multiple smaller changes are often more productive than one large-scale reorganization. Business results always partly depend on existing knowledge, processes, and skills.

---

[*] CCO: Chief Commercial Officer, COO: Chief Operations Officer

Initiatives aimed at significantly improving the quality of the pricing organization rarely succeed in the short term. Making the switch from a subconscious way of working to a situation where board and management never lose sight of pricing, and where all decision drivers accept the rules of the game, will take at least several years.[74] If successful, this switch will make pricing a permanent and appreciated discipline alongside well-established functions, i.e., sales, production, marketing, finance, legal, and HR.

It is in no way certain that this position for pricing is actually attainable at your company. This is often hindered, for instance, because the company fails to turn pricing into a top-3 priority or because there is a lack of unity with regard to pricing within the executive management team and amongst senior managers. Should it prove to be attainable, however, it will be followed by a more gradual development process for expertise, quality, and organization of pricing, which can continue over decades.

12.6 Structure of Part III

The pricing process takes center stage in Chapter 13. We will go into the objective, KPIs, and process steps. We will define the output, and use examples to distinguish subprocesses.

In Chapter 14, we will deal with the attitude of primary functions such as marketing, sales, and finance ("IST"[*]), highlighting the strengths and weaknesses of these departments when it comes to executing pricing tasks.

Chapter 15 will subsequently look at the features of an optimum pricing function ("SOLL"[†]). The nature of the function, deliverables, scope, management, and place within the organization will all be discussed.

---

* "IST": current situation
† "SOLL": targeted future situation

And finally, the focus of Chapter 16 will be on the change aspects that play a role in implementation. We will go into the change approach and change enablers, such as information and the specifics of management resources for the pricing function.

CHAPTER 13

Pricing process

13.1 The pricing factory

The central focus of this chapter is on the pricing process, i.e., the "pricing factory" that sets optimum prices and "produces" commercial conditions for all propositions. Price is the primary driver of revenue and profit. The quality of the pricing process is therefore of crucial importance to financial performance, even though it is far from straightforward to give it a place among all other relevant influences.

In the upcoming sections, we will examine the objective of the pricing process. Following on from that, we will look at quality measurement and key performance indicators, output, throughput, and process levels. We will make a distinction between the strategic, tactical, and operational levels. The organization and change aspects of pricing will be the subject of Chapter 14 and following chapters.

13.2 Objective

The objective of the pricing process is multifaceted. In general terms, the aim is to create an efficient process that produces optimum financial performance. In more specific terms, the process has to meet the following requirements:

1. Effective (business performance)
2. Efficient
3. Speed
4. Customer-friendly
5. Reliable, accurate, and secure
6. Focus
7. Strategically relevant

13.2.1 EFFECTIVE, BUSINESS PERFORMANCE

The pricing process makes a direct contribution to realizing business objectives such as margin, revenue, profit, and market position. It is based on the most relevant price drivers (art) and improves prices through analysis of transparent and verifiable data (science).

13.2.2 EFFICIENT

Efficient execution will cut cost and make cost containable. This happens by making tasks and responsibilities explicit, while also using specialist tools and resources. The costs involved in pricing are often hidden as long as the process is still implicit and costs are spread out. Costs are then incurred in sales processes and financial processes, as well as in the pricing function itself. Employees at different departments dedicate an unknown portion of their time and resources to pricing. Seeing as this keeps these costs out of the CFO's sight, he or she will not perceive any problems. That may make it hard to draw attention to the business case of creating a more efficient pricing process through innovation.

13.2.3 SPEED

The speed of the process is the turnaround time it takes to market a price. This is relevant from a commercial point of view because a shorter turnaround time will produce policy results more quickly. A price change for one product will, of course, have a turnaround time that differs from that of the design of the pricing structure for a market, channel, or product group.

13.2.4 CUSTOMER-FRIENDLY

Clear and friendly communication of prices will enhance customers' perception. They expect correct and easily graspable information about prices, both prior to and after purchasing. It is imperative that customer queries be dealt with fast and adequately. A customer-friendly pricing process is also beneficial for sales staff, as they will be enabled to better focus on the content of the proposition.

13.2.5 RELIABLE, ACCURATE, AND SECURE

Reliability and accuracy are a prerequisite for storage of price-related data and correct calculations during sales phases. The process is secure when sensitive information is treated confidentially during the decision-making process.

13.2.6 FOCUS

The pricing process conveys focus regarding the subject of price to all managers involved across the company. In this context, a shared frame of reference will provide direction to stakeholders. They can thus optimize their contribution to decisions and will not waste time on less relevant discussions. A board that spends a lot of time discussing the win price for a major deal will often lack focus on the pricing process and a sufficiently supported frame of reference for pricing analyses (science) and price drivers (art).

13.2.7 STRATEGICALLY RELEVANT

A company will be able to better address strategic issues when using input from pricing intelligence. If all is well, pricing process performance measurement will also result in appraisal of the effectiveness of the business model, revenue model, and price driver selection.

Pricing can therefore provide estimations of prices, future demand, and revenue *before* strategic changes. This is relevant information during acquisitions, new proposition development, when entering new markets, or when switching to a new business model. In practice, strategists and executives often use input from the pricing manager only as a kind of sanity check *afterwards* instead of as advice *beforehand*.

Imagine, for example, that a company's R&D center has designed a new product. You will in such cases often see that the pricing manager is only asked after the development of the product whether the selling price of the new product is to be €150 or €175. In a strategically relevant pricing process, the pricing manager would have been involved in the development of the product at an earlier stage, so as to assess values of different product development options, as well as whether the selling price should be €350 or perhaps €75.

Another example concerns the takeover of a company. An often seen phenomenon in mergers or acquisitions is that the improvement to the pricing process that is made possible by new market relations is not addressed until after the final closure of the deal. The pricing process is only strategically relevant when it provides input on the future value of integrated pricing *before* the decision to merge with or acquire another company is taken.

13.3 Quality and key performance indicators

The quality of the pricing process depends on the extent to which objectives are attained. Measuring process quality will help management stay in control of the process. The selected KPI will indicate to what degree a process objective has been realized.

When data is not available or a wide range of factors play a role, defining and implementing suitable KPIs can be quite tricky. Popular KPIs for pricing are listed in Table 11. Which KPIs to select depends on the chosen pricing strategy. Short-term profitability, for example, is not as important when the main aim is to build a healthy industry through tacit collusion and price leadership (C8). Margin and customers' value perception have greater importance in a value-driven pricing strategy (C3, C4, and C5). And when the strategy targets financial returns, the level of profit and cost will have greater immediate significance (C1 and C6).

Objective	Commonly used KPIs
1 Effective, higher business performance	▪ Sales volume/revenue/margin ▪ Profitability ▪ Number of users/customers ▪ Revenue/margin per customer ▪ Market share ▪ Market size ▪ Industry-wide price level ▪ Customers' price and value perception
2 Efficient	▪ Direct cost of execution ▪ Cost containability/transparency ▪ Indirect (hidden) costs

3 Speed	▪ Turnaround time
	  – change to pricing strategy
	  – new price lists
	  – price changes
	  – discount request/exception

4 Customer-friendly	▪ Customer satisfaction about price communication ▪ Number of queries from customers ▪ Customer satisfaction about query handling
5 Reliable, accurate, and secure	▪ %, #, and € impact of process errors ▪ # data protection incidents
6 Focus	▪ Quality of decision meetings about price (fact-based, transparency, speed)
7 Strategically relevant	▪ Quality of contribution to strategic decisions (proactive, fact-based, transparency, speed)

Table 11 KPIs for pricing process objectives

13.4 Output

Our definition of the output of the pricing process is as follows:

The pricing process sets and communicates prices and related commercial conditions for products and services a company supplies to customers.

The actual pricing comprises analysis and decision-making processes. Communication of prices across all phases of the sales process is also part of the pricing process. And billing the right net price along with delivery is another component.

The output of pricing is not limited to the gross price, but extends across all discounts and commercial conditions with financial impact. The output therefore encompasses gross price, discounts, net price, payment term, term of delivery, availability and delivery guarantee, and other financial terms and conditions. The underlying basis of the price, sometimes also referred to as the pricing model, is also part of the output. This basis or pricing parameter is used in calculations for the invoice. A telephone call, for example, can be charged *per minute*, and on iTunes, you pay for your music *per track*.

For the sake of maximum clarity of our explanation, this book primarily explains price drivers and price research based on their relevance to the definition of the *level* of the price, while they are equally relevant to the pricing *model*. In some industries, such as software, telecommunications, Internet, or the information industry, the choice of pricing model is of critical importance to the success of a proposition in the market.

13.5 Process levels

The process and its output cover three levels (see Table 12).

Process level	Output	
1 Strategic	Pricing policy	Revenue model, price driver selection, basis of the price, use of price research, tactical and operational process design
	Price guidelines	Target price range, average price and price spread, price positioning, price segmentation and overall direction of price development
2 Tactical	Pricing structure	Gross price list (before any discounts)
	Discount structure	Discount list and/or price promotion policy
	Deal price policy	Guidelines for bespoke prices of individual transactions
3 Operational	Price changes	Short-term changes in price and discount structure for specific elements
	Transaction prices	Net prices offered to customers (after discounts and/or bespoke pricing)

Table 12 Pricing process levels chart

13.6 **Throughput**

The sequence of steps that will get you to the end result is the same on each process level (strategic, tactical, and operational). These steps are depicted in Figure 22.

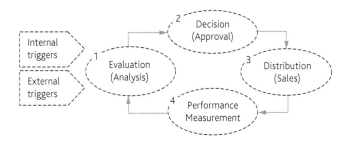

Figure 22 Sequence of steps of the pricing process

The process is triggered by:
- the results of current prices (step 4)
- an internal trigger
- an external trigger

Internal triggers often originate from changes to the commercial policy that lead to a new pricing direction, such as an adjustment of the proposition. External triggers can come from competitors, government policy, or customers.

The evaluation step (1) takes stock of opportunities, risks, and impact of prices. Each process level draws on different sources. On a tactical level, the analysis starts from the strategic guidelines (drivers, use of research and tools, ...). The operational level not only departs from output from the strategic process, but is also based on output on a tactical level (gross pricing structure, discount structure, deal price policy).

Decisions (2) are made on the basis of insights that emerged from the analysis. Authorization processes will come into effect for the decision-making. The difficulty of obtaining formal approval depends on the organizational set-up and scope of the specific pricing decision. Multiple managers and management teams may be involved, with obvious consequences for process speed and quality.

The third step comprises communication and distribution of the price across the sales channels (3). Execution of the sales process with the new prices will determine the company's performance in the market.

The fourth step, i.e., that of performance measurement, will subsequently measure the performance (4), providing input for a new pricing analysis (1), which can produce price adjustments (2).

As shown above, each process level (strategic, tactical, operational) draws on the analysis and data produced by the other levels. The next section will now go into these three process levels in greater detail.

13.7   Strategic pricing process

On a strategic level, the pricing process produces:
1. Pricing policy
2. Price guidelines

The policy sets out the way of working, while the guidelines provide direction in terms of contents. This section will go into both these aspects.

13.7.1 PRICING POLICY

In its pricing policy, a company selects the price drivers it will use (art). Pricing policy stipulates which tools and research methods (science) are to be used, while also capturing best practices and lessons learnt. Policy lays out a roadmap and vision for the development of the pricing function in the medium to long term. It connects pricing to the business strategy and the business model.

Its pricing policy is part of a company's DNA. Not every component of a pricing policy can be changed just like that. Ben & Jerry's and Häagen-Dasz, for example, are ice cream makers with a value-based pricing strategy. It is hard to imagine them as price fighters with reasonable quality ice cream. Like natural organisms, companies change their DNA through step-by-step mutations of one or two elements. Such limited changes may, however, still have a major impact.

The contents of the pricing policy steer activities on every process level. A price fighter will, for example, closely analyze market prices during the operational process. They will adapt prices to market developments to be able to always have low prices (C2 and C4). A premium luxury brand will be more focused on its target group, aligning its prices with perceived value and monitoring price perceptions in their target group (C3, C5, and C7).

13.7.2 PRICE GUIDELINES

Price guidelines provide direction for the level, range, and spread of prices. Price positioning in the market and changes to that positioning for specific segments are laid down on a strategic level. Positioning in the market often depends on a number of competitors who make up the benchmark.* The price distance is the difference

* Benchmark: a standard against which a target variable is compared

between your price and the average price charged by the benchmark group. The policy defines the range within which the price distance is to remain. An oil company, for example, may make the strategic move of charging one cent more than the price leader. On an operational level, it would then update its prices based on this guideline every week.

The range of prices sets the limits within which a company offers its products. Children's pants at a popular department store, for example, sell within a price range from €5 to €25. Price guidelines set a minimum and maximum price for the assortment and the spread of items across different price classes.

Product group Pants - kids

Price classes		No. of items	Relative share
Minimum	Maximum		
€0	€5	0	0%
€5	€10	4	16%
€10	€15	15	60%
€15	€20	5	20%
€20	€25	1	4%
€25	€30	0	0%
€30		0	0%

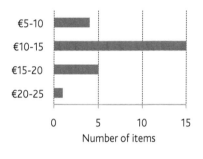

Table 13 Price range and spread for children's pants product group (fictitious data)

The price range in Table 13 goes from €5 up to €25. The emphasis of the collection, however, is on pants priced between €10 and €15. The tactical process sets regular prices for the collection within this guideline.

Retailers use analyses that combine implicit measurements of market prices and sales data (second layer of the FPF) to come up with the best possible strategic guidelines. This is a relatively easy way of obtaining indicators for profitability, customer satisfaction, and market potential for large collections (C1, C3, C4).

Market potential

Price levels in the market will, for example, provide an indication as to the level of demand in each price class. The pricing structure used by competitors tells us where they have identified potential. Competitors' prices can be sourced offline by visiting shops. Online you can use web robots. These robots monitor prices at online shops and store these in a database.

The extent to which competitors are successful thanks to their pricing can be assessed based on buying behavior data. Market research firms are in the business of compiling detailed overviews of spending per price class per type of retailer based on consumer panel research. The market value of each price class can be deduced from that information.

Profitability

Using sales data, you can analyze past performance in every price class. Revenue generated by pants priced between €5 and €10 in previous seasons provides an indication of what performance will be like in the coming season. The best results are achieved when you combine these implicit measurements with category managers' expert judgment (first layer of the FPF). A buyer or category manager will be tuned in to consumer trends. They will have certain expectations in terms of the performance of (new) items in a collection based on product-intrinsic grounds.

When comparing the performance of price classes, two effects will play opposite roles. Cheaper items will generally generate:
- greater volume
- lower absolute per-unit margins

Performance is helped by greater volumes sold, but hindered by low margins. Items in the bottom half of the price range often generate volume, while expensive items bring in higher per-unit margins. A pair of children's pants that sells for €18 may, for example, have been procured by the retailer for €7. Another pair of children's pants was purchased for €5 and sells for €12. The absolute margin of €11 for the more expensive pair is higher than the €7 margin on the other pair.

The cheaper pair of pants can only justify its place in the store when it manages to rack up a sales volume that is over one-and-a-half times that of the more expensive pair (11:7).

Table 14 provides an example of a performance analysis. The absolute margin per item shows the returns generated by the sales of an item. It is the amount you earn by having the item in your assortment.[*] This margin is the product of the two abovementioned variables:

- number of items sold
- absolute per-unit margin

Product group Pants – kids

| Price classes | | Last year's returns (averages) | | | | | New price range | |
Min	Max	No. of items	Relative share	Volume /item	€ margin /unit	€ margin /item	No. of items	Relative share
€5	€10	8	33%	52,557	€4.70	€247,018	4	16%
€10	€15	13	54%	45,203	€7.10	€320,941	15	60%
€15	€20	3	13%	37,329	€11.89	€443,842	5	20%
€20	€25	0	0%				1	4%

Table 14 Analysis of returns on guidelines for price range of children's pants (fictitious data)

The average *volume per item* amounts to 52,557 units in the bottom price class (€5-€10). This volume trumps that of all other price classes. The average *per-unit margin*, however, is highest in the price class from €15 to €20. This margin is €11.89, over twice that of the €5 to €10 price class. The high volume for the lowest price class cannot make up for this high margin per unit. The absolute *per-item margin* is therefore higher for the higher price classes: €443,842 for the highest price class and €320,941 for the price class from €10 to €25. The new price range (see Figure 23) will take that into consideration. There is a greater supply of items in the higher price classes.

Figure 23 reflects the shift by offsetting last year's range against this year's, with the latter based on new strategic price range guidelines.

---

[*] Within the same product group, this matches net revenue per square foot of floor space, which is an important benchmark for retailers.

Category managers, product managers, and buyers have changed the composition and prices of the children's pants collection based on these new guidelines.

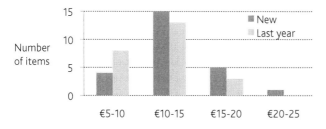

Figure 23 New price range compared to last year's (fictitious data)

13.8 Tactical pricing process

On a tactical level, the pricing process produces:
1. Pricing structure
2. Discount structure and price promotion policy
3. Deal price policy

The pricing structure specifies regular prices. The discount structure contains discounts, often given on certain volumes. The price promotion policy specifies the tactical deployment of price discounts. The deal price policy sets guidelines for transaction price customization. This section will cover all three tactical pricing process products, and use an elaborate example to address the effectiveness of different kinds of discounts.

13.8.1 PRICING STRUCTURE

The tactical pricing process determines the pricing structure, the so-called gross prices. These are the regular prices for all products, services, and propositions, as listed on the price list. There are many different names for the standard price list, such as the price book or rate structure.

The price list is an important table for companies, because it contains information that is not only relevant to the pricing process. This table is used by various primary processes. The sales process consults the price table in compiling offers and advising customers. Supply chain processes manage stock and logistics based on the price list. And production processes and financial processes also use gross prices as a source.

13.8.2 DISCOUNT STRUCTURE AND PRICE PROMOTION POLICY

Many sectors give discounts on standard prices. In B2B, customers who purchase large quantities often qualify for a volume discount. Manufacturers of consumer goods also reward retailers with better terms and conditions when they purchase more. The discount structure determines when customers qualify for a discount, and how much the discount will be. The price promotion policy describes how price reductions can be used tactically to help reach (short-term) business objectives.

Which discount or price promotion works best differs based on the objective and the market. Price drivers such as communication (C7) and cross-selling (C10) play significant roles in this context. We will illustrate the effectiveness of different kinds of discount by way of an example.

13.8.3 OPTIMIZING PRICE PROMOTIONS

Retailers and consumer goods manufacturers have devised a multitude of price promotions. The specific objectives they seek to realize with these promotions therefore also differ considerably per promotion, depending on the reason for offering the promotion. There are four primary business objectives underlying a promotion, aimed at improving:

- sales volume
- revenue
- margin
- stock position

And there are also secondary objectives, which seek to stimulate or improve:

- footfall
- conversion[*]
- cross-selling
- new customers
- trials
- customer satisfaction
- price perception

The price promotion policy specifies how discounts are to be used. It stipulates which type of price promotion is to be used for the objective it is supposed to achieve, and also defines the selected format and intended communication channels (media). The policy determines whether and how a business case is to be made for each promotion, which would assess additional revenue and margin, realized discounts, and cost of execution. This budget will be the point of reference for the performance measurement afterwards. Measuring side effects, such as footfall, cross-selling, conversion, and the like, will lead to better understanding of the effects. Knowledge of the effects of promotions will thus grow steadily.

We can distinguish the following types of promotion:

- A *direct benefit* in the form of a discount on the price versus an *indirect benefit*
- More volume of *the same product* for free versus *other products* for free
- Benefit *upon purchase* versus benefit *in the future*
- *Freely available* benefits versus *restricted*[†] benefits

We will briefly go into the functioning of four price promotions:

a. direct price discount
b. volume discount
c. discount at another supplier
d. discount in the future

---

[*] Percentage of visitors that proceeds to purchase
[†] Per customer, product, shop shelf, shop, channel, time of booking/delivery/use

For each of these four versions, you can furthermore opt for unlimited or restricted availability of the discount.

a. direct price discount

Offering a direct discount on the price is an obvious type of price promotion. There are three formats that can be used to communicate such a direct discount on the price:

Figure 24 Three direct price discount formats

For small price tags, it is best to express discounts as a percentage (format 1). At supermarkets, shoppers are often overwhelmed by percentage discounts. 30% off on a bag of crisps is just more impressive than a €0.30 discount. Behavior experiments have shown that people sooner specifically go to a shop for a large percentage discount on one cheap item than for a discount of the same *amount* on a more expensive item. They'd rather save $7 on a $25 pen than $7 on a $455 suit.[75]

When the price promotion is greater, in an absolute sense, formats 2 and 3 are better suited. When exactly a price promotion becomes a large one is impossible to say beforehand. Testing formats and analyzing their effects is the best way of selecting one of the options. And when you cannot decide on a format, combinations of different formats will offer a way out, so you can use both signs reading "from €99, now €69" and signs reading "30% discount". Combining formats is also beneficial when a large number of products have been marked down. Retailers often use generic discount promises such as "up to 50% off" and "up to €75 off" in their shops and shop windows. This has a positive effect on consumers' price perception. It stimulates footfall and sales of items with smaller markdowns.

Advantages of direct price discount

Due to their transparency, direct price discounts are a stronger purchase trigger for customers. Footfall receives a relatively big boost. The greater the number of items in the assortment that are marked down, the greater that effect.

Disadvantages of direct price discount

Its transparency also makes direct price discounting an expensive form of promotion. Other types of promotion often make a discount seem bigger than it really is. A direct discount does not. Table 15 shows the volume increase that is needed to generate the same revenue and maintain the same absolute margin (revenue minus purchase costs) after a price discount.

Price discount	Extra volume required for same revenue	Extra volume required for same absolute margin
10%	11%	25%
20%	25%	67%
30%	43%	150%
40%	67%	400%
50%	100%	Impossible
60%	150%	Impossible
70%	233%	Impossible
Procurement costs: 50% of original pre-tax selling price		

Table 15 Sales volume increases required to keep revenue or margin steady when discounting

What we can infer from this is that it is hard to increase revenue or margins when you give big discounts. The table is based on purchase costs that amount to 50% of the pre-tax selling price level.[*] The smaller the variable margin, the more items you need to sell to justify price discounts.

Another drawback is that a direct discount is not explicitly intended to incentivize customers to buy larger volumes. And its transparency

---

[*] The selling price that consumers pay may include sales tax. The price discount will reduce both selling price and pre-tax selling price level by the same percentage.

will also enable competitors to respond quicker, bringing the unwelcome risk of price erosion. The transparency of discounts sends a signal to consumers saying that the normal price is too high. This undermines price perception.

b. volume discount

This is a discount that is given when you purchase a larger quantity. Stores often use the following formats for this kind of discount (see Figure 25):

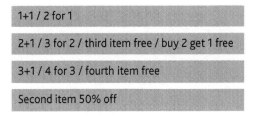

1+1 / 2 for 1
2+1 / 3 for 2 / third item free / buy 2 get 1 free
3+1 / 4 for 3 / fourth item free
Second item 50% off

Figure 25 Four volume discount formats

The offer of "third item free" creates the perception of a 33% discount. The actual discount is lower, because the *cheapest* of the three items will be free. The average discount of a 2+1 promotion may be 25% instead of 33%, and the average discount of a 1+1 promotion could very well be 40% instead of the insinuated 50%.

A volume discount incites customers to buy more. After all, they only get a discount when they buy a larger quantity. Table 15 showed that sales volume would need to rise considerably for a price promotion to pay off. And this greater sales volume is exactly what a volume discount brings.

One drawback is that regular customers will accumulate a large supply, which will cause revenue to slump in the long term. Aside from that, volume discounts are relatively less appealing to new customers. They often want to try out a product or service first before they start purchasing large quantities.

c. Discount at another supplier

Giving a discount on a product at another store will often make a very positive impression. Getting a product that normally costs €50 for free gives consumers the perception of having bagged a €50 windfall. The actual costs are generally lower than this insinuated gain. The product that consumers get for free in this deal will, after all, be procured smartly and in large volumes. And there will also be customers who do not take advantage of the promotion.[*] The free product on offer must appeal to the target group. Retailers therefore often use well-known brands or products as the complimentary item in such promotions.

There are numerous ways of executing this price promotion. One example is that of an energy company that gives customers a voucher for a discount when they enter into a supply contract for gas and electricity. This voucher entitles the new customer to a €75 discount on shoes from a fast-growing online shoe store. Both companies stand to gain something from the promotion. The energy company attracts new customers relatively cheaply. The actual costs of the voucher are a fraction of the €75 face value. And the online shop can welcome a large number of new customers by hitching a ride on the energy supplier's large-scale marketing wagon.

d. discount in the future

The types of discount we have discussed so far are given right there and then at the moment of purchase. A discount in the future either gives customers the prospect of a windfall the next time they buy something or allows them to save up for rewards. This type of discounting is attractive because it encourages customers to return. Its influence on price perception is also positive. A voucher for a 10% discount on the next purchase leads customers to believe they will get 10% off. In reality, however, you have to make two purchases to get a 10% discount once. The average discount is therefore 5%. It results in a higher margin.

---

[*] Redemption rate: % customers taking advantage of the promotion, which is often well below 100%.

Schemes that allow customers to save up for rewards also provide benefits in the future. One attractive aspect of rewards schemes is that they focus customers' attention on the *activity* of saving instead of on the exact financial gain. Shell was successful in the Netherlands with its scheme that allowed customers to save up coupons that they could eventually exchange for towels. Supermarket chain Albert Heijn runs a campaign whereby shoppers receive free stickers for every 10 euros spent at one of their stores. Themed on a wide range of subjects, such as football or animals, these stickers are hugely popular with children, who pressure their parents into getting all their groceries at Albert Heijn.

These rewards schemes have one common denominator: they cost the retailer a fraction of the revenue customers chasing those rewards bring in. Achieving the same level of loyalty through direct discounts would be a far more costly undertaking.

13.8.4 DEAL PRICE POLICY

A deal price policy or custom pricing policy is a policy on offers that deviate from the regular pricing and discount structure. These offers are always customized, leaving plenty of leeway in formulating individual deals.

There are various reasons why customization is needed sometimes. Customers may issue requests for proposal that dictate the price parameters. Or a sales pitch may leave room for price customization, or transactions may be relatively important. Generally accepted principles in a specific industry can also play a role. Major clients of IT service providers, for example, generally want customized solutions. In consumer markets, kitchen sellers and car dealers use specific policies in coming to a net price they can offer potential customers in a sales talk.

On a tactical level, the deal price policy produces guidelines for price deals and the value proposition for different types of customers and different kinds of solutions. And it also stipulates the method and templates for the transaction process.

On an operational level, customized offers often require a business case with a forecast of income and expenditure. Based on that business case, the offer can then be approved. The deal price policy specifies the format, definitions, parameters, and guidelines for the business case. This aids consistency and speed of the execution of the operational process.

13.9 Operational pricing process

On an operational level, the pricing process produces:
1. Price changes
2. Transaction prices

Price changes are incidental and limited changes to the pricing structure. In setting transaction prices, pricing policy and pricing structure are applied for each individual sale. This section will go into both components.

13.9.1 PRICE CHANGES

The tactical level compiles a price list or discount structure following a steady rhythm, departing from a new strategy or in response to external developments. The operational pricing process subsequently defines the changes to individual prices, for example because demand for a certain product has suddenly dropped, or because a competitor wins a large market share in one customer segment. That will necessitate limited changes to the price or discount list.

"Price watch" processes are on the lookout for external and internal signals that suggest that such changes are needed. Important triggers that would need to be monitored are competitors' prices, margins, and sales volumes. Price watching can be a state-of-the-art operation when using software that scans competitors' prices online and subsequently automatically adjusts prices.

13.9.2 TRANSACTION PRICES

The transaction pricing process sets net prices that customers will be charged and defines them in agreements made during the sale of products and services. The process ensures that these agreements are in line with the pricing and discount structure and the deal price policy. And it also produces, within the order-to-invoice process, the amount due and its breakdown on the invoice.

Administrative execution

Depending on the guidelines on a tactical level, execution of this process may be complex. Sales staff and administrative employees are responsible for putting it into practice, but they often lack training in the realm of pricing. And the IT systems that are used were often not developed with strategic pricing requirements in mind. Errors in this process are costly: amounts due on an invoice that are too high or incomprehensible invoices lead to discontented customers and laborious credit notes. And an invoice amount that is too low leads to a loss of margin.

Precisely in the implementation of carefully considered pricing methods, the quality of the operational execution is of crucial importance. So what is needed is training of employees who are responsible for execution, installation, and configuration of IT systems such as ERP[*] and CRM,[†] checking for errors in output, and attention to customer responses.

Authorization and decision-making

The deal price policy defines the model and strategy of the analysis of the business case that is required for approval of customized offers. On an operational level, sales and financial staff must be familiarized with the terminology, strategy, and business concepts.

---

[*] ERP: Enterprise Resource Planning. This is software for the management of production and logistics (supply chain).

[†] CRM: Customer Relationship Management. This is software for management and commercial use of all customer information.

Evaluation of (potential) transactions adheres to the tactical guidelines. The approval process defines authorizations, while also offering flexibility and speed and providing a clear mandate for the sales talk.

Performance measurement
The transaction pricing process supplies data for performance analysis on all process levels. Win/loss data, for example, indicates how successful the sales proposition and pricing are. This is, however, conditional on a clear and well-structured database of past offers being available. Giving discounts also produces useful information, providing all discount elements can be identified. Pocket-price waterfall analyses enable better underpinning of discount structures (see Figure 26).[76]

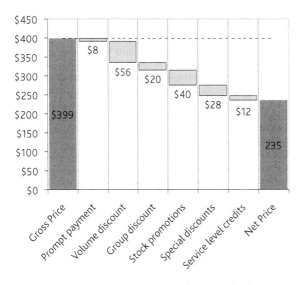

Figure 26 Example of discounts in B2B (fictitious data)

CHAPTER 14
Internal perspectives

14.1 Price as second priority

Only in exceptional cases does pricing receive specific attention in the organizational set-up of companies. The various pricing-related tasks are usually performed by different departments. One department will often outrank the others in the pricing stakes, but it cannot come to decisions about pricing without the collaboration or even approval of other sections of the company. Centralized direction for optimum decision-making and efficient process is therefore lacking.

An important reason underlying this lack of attention for pricing is that pricing is never the first priority of the department that is primarily responsible for it. At product management and marketing, product and communication take center stage. Sales' first priority is to generate sales and revenue. Category management predominantly focuses on sourcing and composition of the product range. At the finance department, the prime concern is financial reporting, management information, investment analysis, and capital transactions. At the operational departments of the company, delivery and production take precedence. The board, finally, lacks oversight when it comes to pricing, and is largely clueless about the absence of coordination lower down in the organization. Lacking detailed knowledge, it is unable to seize pricing opportunities. Consequently, strategy is not converted into implementation.

This chapter will go into the perspectives of all the departments listed above. This will lead to an "IST" description[*] of the implicit, less conscious, behavior toward price. Chapter 15 will subsequently focus on the features of a well-considered and soundly organized pricing function.

14.2 Marketing

14.2.1 COMPONENTS OF MARKETING

The marketing domain explicitly claims price management as one of its duties by including it in the famous 4 Ps of the marketing mix:[77]
- product
- place
- promotion
- price

It is always a challenge for marketers to cover the ambitious scope of their profession. And price happens to be the most difficult component of their scope.

Good *product* managers or brand managers have a strategic, creative, and communicative attitude. They tailor products and services to the preferences of customers, in consultation with architects and engineers from production and R&D departments. They develop a brand that ties in with their target group's perception. "Marcom"[†] translates this perception and the strengths of the products into *promotional* material or, in the case of some online applications, a dialogue about the brand. Marcom teams up with advertising agencies, copywriters, and visual experts. As the final step in the process, marketing distribution managers see to delivery to the right *place* through all channels.

---

* IST: the situation as it is now (Ch.14); SOLL: as it should be (Ch.15)
† Marcom: marketing communication

Often *pricing* is handled by product managers. But price to them is the final piece of a long and busy day. This sometimes prompts marketing directors to set up a dedicated pricing team, which subsequently works independently from the product managers. The analyses for pricing (science) and the creative thinking that is needed to refine price drivers (art) are not the kind of activities that seamlessly slot into product management's day-to-day work. And the activities of product management, such as branding and defining specifications, only provide part of the input needed for pricing. Although the make-up of the product and service range partly determines customer value, setting optimum prices requires more work.

14.2.2 QUANTITATIVE SKILLS

Product, place, and promotion primarily call for high-quality understanding of the market, customers, and business opportunities for the company. Many product managers can boast many years of experience in their industry. They know both product and service specifications and customer expectations inside out.

But quantitative insight is equally indispensable for pricing. Marketers often lack the ability to compare price alternatives on the right financial basis and perform complex calculations. They struggle to quantify possible responses from customers and run sound research into that. Marketers are not fond of detailed figures, and neither do they like concretizing concepts behind the single figure that price is at first sight. A view of the bigger financial picture is enough to get the best product in the right place with a powerful promotional message. Attention to detailed figures is, however, essential in maximizing revenue through optimum pricing. The devil is in the detail.

One example of the right way of going about it are the specialist pricing teams at mobile telecommunications companies, which meticulously and comprehensively weigh up possible pricing models against each other.

Vodafone,[78] for example, charges a standard rate of 71 cents per minute for calls to Germany. It does not charge any additional costs per call. Some of its customers, however, may find this expensive. For these customers, Vodafone has a value plan. Customers who sign up to the "international calls+texts" scheme by sending a text message will pay 30 cents per minute and 79 cents per call (see Table 16).

Rates	Standard rate	Value plan	Benefit %
per minute	€0.71	€0.30	58%
per call	€0.00	€0.79	NA

Table 16 Vodafone's charges for an international call from the Netherlands to Germany

Consumers who dislike the standard rate of 71 cents are happy with the 58% lower per-minute rate of 30 cents offered by the value plan. However, calls are often about 2 to 3 minutes long. The actual gain is therefore below 58%, and lies somewhere between 2% and 21% for a 2 or 3-minute call (see Table 17). This way Vodafone still realizes reasonable returns on value plan customers.

Charge per call	Standard rate	Value plan	Benefit %
1 minute	€0.71	€1.09	−54%
2 minutes	€1.42	€1.39	2%
3 minutes	€2.13	€1.69	21%

Table 17 Call charges based on (i) standard rate (ii) "international calls+texts" value plan

14.3   Sales

14.3.1   CUSTOMER-CENTRIC

The idea behind sales departments enjoying (greater) freedom in setting prices is that this is supposed to make them more customer-centric. This greater focus on customers produces better results when prices are customized (C5) and customers want to negotiate a price on the spot. Autonomy for sales staff and deal makers speeds up the decision-making process. It also opens up an opportunity to better exploit interactions with customers. This aids customer satisfaction and increases efficiency and effectiveness of both pricing and sales. Sales staff is expected to use their (partial) mandate for pricing to achieve greater margins "whenever possible" and charge a lower price "whenever necessary".

14.3.2 PRICE AS A WEAPON

In practice, sales departments see price as a *weapon* in attracting customers. Board members consider it dangerous and unwanted to release such a powerful weapon among sales staff. In their eyes, the availability of a weapon will lead to the use of that weapon. They fear the negative consequences for the business' financial health. What causes the aggressiveness sales staff display in deploying the weapon of price is often their personal bonus, which is not in line with the company's objective. The prospect of a revenue-based bonus for the salesman turns price into a deadly weapon when what the company needs are higher margins and profits instead of higher revenue.

In trying to hit revenue-based targets, sales managers tend to give additional discounts to incite customers to buy. A salesperson will prefer a *sure* deal with 10% less revenue over the *risk* of rejection. For the company, however, the scales may tip in the opposite direction. A price that is 10% lower will reduce revenue by 10%, but may hurt the much-needed margin considerably more.

Many boards find it hard to align targets for sales staff with those for the company as a whole. This alignment requires conversion of annual business targets at overall company level into targets for customers on the level of relationships or individual transactions. That requires guidelines to facilitate the rather subjective calculation of variable and fixed costs (also refer to 2.2.2) in every offer. Implementation processes will be delayed when finance managers are fixated on calculating costs truthfully and in detail before the authority of commercial managers is extended. These conscientious financial employees lose sight of the objective of what they are doing, i.e., aligning business targets with those of sales staff. This is far easier to do with relatively loosely estimated limits for costs and margins, such as based on gross prices or a simplified cost structure.

14.3.3 STRUCTURE IN PRICES

A second downside of price autonomy for the sales department is that this department is generally short on skills when it comes to managing structure and analytical thought. This is a downside because only structural processing of data will enable better tailoring to customer preferences and more efficient process execution. The deployment of pricing science produces prices that match customer value. The set-up, analysis, and use of information[*] about customers, market shares, costs, and competitive prices benefit from centralization. And a clear and unequivocal structure in the administration of prices and discounts will boost the integrity of operational processes such as billing and accounts receivable management.

A pricing team benefits from an autonomous set-up of its activities. This calls for clear boundaries and management of day-to-day commercial operations. A disadvantage of individual sales staff members having the authority to autonomously make decisions about prices is that it will make it harder to set up structures and pricing intelligence. Sales staff is less inclined to share knowledge about customers, market, and prices. Restricting the mandate of sales and streamlining communication between sales staff and the pricing team, however, could yield a great wealth of data "from the field".

14.3.4 FOCUS ON VALUE FOR CUSTOMERS

Sales adds value when this department can focus on the unique selling points of the proposition and customers' specific preferences. When you give sales managers the authority to negotiate prices, this focus is often lost. If they are not authorized to make price decisions, sales staff will work to raise the perceived value in their sales talks by listening to customers' buying motives and tapping into those, instead of picking customers up on their attempts to enter into price negotiations.

---

* Also refer to Part II The Science of Pricing

14.4   Marketing and sales

14.4.1   SPLIT MANDATE

Authority over pricing matters is often shared by sales and marketing. Marketing will then, for example, compile gross price lists and a standard discount structure. Sales has considerable freedom to stray from these lists and structures in individual cases "if necessary".

14.4.2   LACK OF CONTROL

Splitting the mandate for pricing decisions between marketing and sales comes with all the drawbacks listed in the sections on marketing (14.2) and sales (14.3). And an additional disadvantage is that it leads to a significant lack of control. Neither sales, nor marketing has a clear view of the net price customers pay or of how the price relates to the perceived value and market prices. After all, both departments only oversee part of the pricing process.

14.4.3   ATTITUDE OF MARKETING AND SALES

The strength of marketing managers and sales managers often lies in their proactive attitude. They have an ability to be creative with prices and in the implementation of the pricing strategy as part of a commercial approach. Their thinking is focused on the future. This is productive for pricing, as the consequences of price decisions reveal themselves in the future and are by definition unpredictable. These managers, however, often lack the ability to quantify insights, assess alternatives, or structure analyses and processes.

14.5   Category management

14.5.1   LINCHPIN

In retail and wholesale, buying or merchandising is in charge of strategic decisions. This is the department that decides which products the company buys and sells. It is responsible for procurement and stocks. It sets prices and the policy for promotions, including price discounts and special offers.

Nowadays, retailers also have a separate function in their organization called "category management", which puts together the assortment. Promotions policy, stock management, vendor selection, and negotiations are the responsibility of departments such as marketing communication, supply chain, and sourcing. Category management is in charge of the assortment and prices, in the spirit of buyers' exploits in this realm.

The role of merchandising as the linchpin in commercial processes suits the multitude of information that is needed for a pricing policy and operational optimization of price changes and discounts.

14.5.2   ATTITUDE OF CATEGORY MANAGEMENT

It is difficult for a category management department to have a clear idea of the customer and understand value perception. Its focus is more on costs and manufacturers than on customers. Category managers or buyers are proactive and future-oriented, but their priority lies with putting together the assortment and not with pricing opportunities. They look after the bottom line, look at quality, and only focus specific attention on the top 10 of articles from the assortment. Opportunities for better prices generally emerge from an analysis of the entire price portfolio and detailed additional information about customers, market, and competitors. Most category managers or merchandisers do not have this attention to detail.

14.6   Finance

14.6.1   WATCHDOG

Traditionally, the CFO is the person guarding a company's financial health. Finance is responsible for reporting, accounting, and other administrative matters. This is also the department that works on attracting capital and appraising investments.

14.6.2 INFORMATION PROVISION

Back in the days when the world did not turn as fast as it does today, a true and fair reflection of a company's affairs in an annual report was enough in terms of information provision. But in today's world, ambitions and requirements have gone beyond that. Financial controllers produce a multitude of analyses and reports to support business functions. Data warehouses provide central and accessible storage of performance data. Dashboards with key performance indicators display the status of processes.

14.6.3 CHECKS AFTERWARDS

CFOs feel responsible for pricing whenever it comes up, but they struggle with the actual pricing process. The differences between the various price drivers are often unknown to them. Financial managers are not used to taking a creative approach to business models, customer needs, and pricing strategies.

In B2B markets, the finance department often counterbalances sales and marketing managers' relatively liberal approach to price. When rewards for individual sales staff members and business targets are misaligned, these companies may miss out on a great deal of margin. This would be the case when incentives for sales staff are uniquely focused on landing orders (see Section 14.3.2). Finance's role is then a controlling one, because it has to approve offers. The fact that offers have to be run by finance gives finance the chance to monitor margins, although it doesn't itself have any means of maximizing margins.

All the efforts of the sales team are targeted on maximizing the chance of landing an order. Draft offers often only make it to the financial department for approval at a late stage, close to the date on which the offer is to be sent to the potential customer. Under pressure of time, what the finance department will look at is whether the offer generates *sufficient* margin and whether the pitched price is *low enough* for the customer. Opportunities to *maximize* the margin by using a different deal strategy or solution approach have then basically already been lost: there is no time to work out a new approach. The offer still has to be signed by the board and the proposal needs to be with the customer tomorrow to meet the deadline specified in the RFP.

14.6.4 ATTITUDE OF FINANCE

In this day and age, the finance department's relevance to marketing, sales, category management, and production is greater than it used to be. But the traditional traits of this department have nonetheless been preserved in their basic attitude. A financial manager works on verification, analysis, and monitoring based on facts from the past that help him come to a definite answer on the correctness of a decision.

Finance staff's behavior when it comes to the pricing policy is generally one of wait and see. They limit themselves to reactively analyzing proposals formulated by others. Whenever the annual financial reporting cycle is guzzling time and resources, the CFO will prioritize these formal financial management activities, which goes at the expense of the development of a timely and accurate pricing process for customers.

14.7 Operations and production

14.7.1 COST EXPERTISE

Details about the cost price are the domain of operational managers and analysts. They are familiar with the cost elements that fall within the scope of the operations department, simply because they need that data to be able to optimize processes. Production management can offset estimations against actual results. They can also rely on understanding of what costs are made up of, as they work to improve cost levels in the short, medium, and long term.

Operational staff has a tendency to mistake selling price for cost price and vice versa. Price is often equated with cost price. And they talk about the selling price as the cost price plus a mark-up "for the margin". The ability to identify opportunities for better prices through the use of different price drivers is only available in these circles to a limited degree.

14.7.2 FEARS

Operational managers have several fears when it comes to price, such as the fear of sales selling products too cheaply or "giving them away". Another possible fear is that of a sister operation paying the production unit a transfer price that is too low. And they sometimes think that if sales, finance, or the board were to know all the ins and outs of the costs, this would lead to them meddling in the operational organization. In their view, these outsiders have insufficient grasp of the complexity and mutual dependency of the activities. It then seems better to withhold certain information: the operations department would rather lead the blind than meddlers with limited sight.

14.7.3 COST TRANSPARENCY

Proper use of price drivers requires understanding of costs. The detailed cost information that the operations department possesses will therefore really have to come out into the open. Cost-to-serve plays a critical role in price customization (C5, C6). A cost leadership strategy (C2) or fighting a cost leader in the battle with competitors (C3, C4) calls for insight into (uncertain) developments of costs in the future.

It is not easy for pricing managers to get that level of transparency from the operations department. The first steps toward a better pricing policy are generally taken in the realms of marketing and sales. Pricing managers then give lower priority to a better understanding of operations, which they may come to regret in the long term.

14.7.4 ATTITUDE OF OPERATIONS

The operations department can rely on a reasonably sound understanding of quantitative issues. Their attitude toward (cost) price is analytical and focused on control. Creativity in relation to business models and (selling) price strategy is a quality you will not easily find in a company's operational circles.

Possible objections to innovation of price drivers can, with some perseverance, be dispelled effectively. Operational managers appreciate an explanation that focuses on content. Without such an explanation, they may hold back innovative strategies for drivers such as customization (C5, C6), cross-selling (C10), and co-selling (C11).

14.8 Board

14.8.1 LEADERSHIP

All business functions converge in the board of directors. The attitude of the CEO is decisive. He may, in his role of entrepreneur, take pricing matters into his own hands, or exercise strict oversight of pricing. Often, a CEO will delegate parts of this responsibility to the CFO, CCO, or a COO with a broader set of duties.

Who takes the lead when it comes to pricing is often less well defined. The pricing process is partly organized on a subconscious level. Tasks, processes, resources, and consultations between departments remain out of the board's line of sight. Structural policy about prices is lacking.

There is no business plan for pricing in the long term. The pricing strategy has not been formulated accurately, and offers no concrete basis for pricing and discounting. A dashboard and KPI measurement for pricing processes are lacking. Discussions about price at board meetings are incidental and reactive. Measures agreed by the board merely tackle symptoms and do not show a deeper understanding of the consequences of their choices for the business model or the industry.

It is not easy for a board to show leadership on this subject in these circumstances. It therefore normally passes the buck to one of their colleagues, such as the Chief Commercial Officer or the CFO.

14.8.2 UNITY

As soon as this newly assigned owner of the pricing initiative gets to work with great enthusiasm, he or she will often come up against more resistance than expected. He or she will be faced with peculiar counter-productive reactions, not only from other business functions, but also from middle managers at his or her own department. What this colleague, who has been put in charge of taking the initiative on pricing, needs is the backing of a board that stands united. But still, any board will be handicapped by a lack of knowledge of the possibilities of pricing in this situation.

14.8.3 ATTITUDE OF THE BOARD

Owing to the fact that boards of directors maintain a certain distance from day-to-day affairs, and are responsible for the company as a whole, they often assume a creative and future-driven approach to business development. This is in keeping with their duty of defining the pricing strategy. Most board members, however, do not have the experience required to strategically deploy the price tool. And the ability to quantify a vision to the level of detail that pricing requires is also lacking on boards. Leadership in pricing matters is a huge challenge for the C-suite at many companies.

14.9 Pricing authority

Which department takes the lead when it comes to prices depends on the organizational structure of the company and the industry. It is likely to be a department that is considered a "strong" one internally. On the implementation side, it will be the department that is in charge of the contents of the commercial proposition with a role as the linchpin in commercial processes.

Marketers generally call the shots at consumer goods manufacturers. They define the contents of the marketing mix and take the lead on prices. In retail and the wholesale trade, merchandising or category management takes the lead. Sales has maximum pricing authority in B2B environments, where customers receive a tailored service. Finance is often a strong gatekeeper.

At first glance, it *seems* advisable to put or keep these departments who have already taken the lead in charge of pricing. After all, their position gives them the best overview of all factors. There is however the danger of pricing receiving insufficient attention, as numerous other tasks distract the linchpin role's focus away from pricing. And there is limited willingness to own up to mistakes and learn from them. Being a prominent department internally, criticism is often unwelcome due to the many interests at stake.

Having a leading business function that takes on the subject and acts as an operational driving force behind projects is what makes or breaks the first improvements to the pricing function. Successes in the realm of pricing policy are only possible through collaboration with this department that is in the lead. One challenge is, though, the initial lack of pricing expertise: improvements are slow going.

Actual progress is conditional on the company having an independent pricing function, which is also represented on the board. In the next chapter, we will describe the kind of pricing function that is required, and the leadership needed for that.

CHAPTER 15

Pricing function

15.1 Unity

The previous chapter outlined regular business functions' perspectives on pricing ("IST"). This chapter will now show how the pricing function should ideally be set up ("SOLL").

The explicit organizational set-up for pricing aims to unify policy and execution. Price would then no longer be a forgotten, nearly external factor, but a clearly addressed and critical control variable. It would mean management of the company has control of the pricing function, using pricing policy to attain strategic objectives. The pricing function would integrate all considerations and data to produce the best possible pricing structure. Information and communication technology would further facilitate the creation of separate pricing departments that can better execute the science of pricing.

This chapter will first go into the orientation and approach of the pricing team, and subsequently discuss the scope of the pricing function, management of prices, and integration into the organization. In this context, leadership from the Chief Pricing Officer role is crucial for major corporations that are made up of multiple business units.

15.2 Orientation

Two antitheses provide a clear indication of the extent to which the approach and orientation of the pricing function differ from those of regular departments, namely:

1. quality versus quantity
2. control versus freedom

15.2.1 QUALITY VERSUS QUANTITY

Managers who go by quality and case histories can make policy based on only one example. "One exception to the rule is a pilot, two exceptions are a new rule." This quip about special customer conditions at a sales department betrays how policy is made. Managers with a quality-based approach tend to use comprehensive narrative and visualizations to show *how* and *why* their proposals will bring success. They are curious about the details behind individual cases and draw structural improvements from those cases.

Managers who are oriented on quantity prefer to analyze all information about customers, markets, and products. Quantifying their findings, they arrive at the best possible choices by weighing up statistics. They have a great knack of converting considerations into policy and prices. Their understanding of the cold reality behind the figures, however, is less impressive.

Pricing managers like to work in a quantitative and data-driven way. Although they do use qualitative input from sales and marketing,* they add value in that they actually assess the implications of business cases and pricing models and underpin them with data. When pricing managers join commercial managers in their creative approach, their role is to compare options in a quantitative sense and guard the structure of price propositions.

---

* Also refer to the layer of expert judgment in Part II – The Science of Pricing

Results can be achieved through strict adherence to rules and control, but also by following the inspiration that comes with freedom. These two extremes are the second dimension we will use to describe the orientation of pricing.

Rules and control are productive ways of guarding structure, facilitating accountability, and creating a sense of certainty. The question which rules to use is answered based on past successes. Data derived from past experiences will certainly come in handy when rendering account and safeguarding the health of the company. But the pricing function calls for a more creative approach and the ability to make choices from a position of uncertainty. This is the other end of the spectrum: an approach of working in freedom, focused on the future, whereby choices are based on uncertain premises.

The effects of pricing decisions emerge in the future. Although analysis of past successes and failure is a valid way of obtaining grounding for choices, the fact of the matter is that "past results do not guarantee future performance".

15.2.3 **THE ATTITUDE OF PRICING**

So how exactly does the pricing function relate to other, more established, business functions (see Ch. 14) in the two above-described dimensions? We have compared them to each other in Figure 27.

The commercial functions of sales, marketing, and category management appear in the top-right quadrant. They base themselves on quality and are creative, as well as future-driven. Their aim is to tap customer preferences and developments in the market. Finance and operations, on the other hand, are better at controlled execution of processes. Finance has a highly quantitative focus.

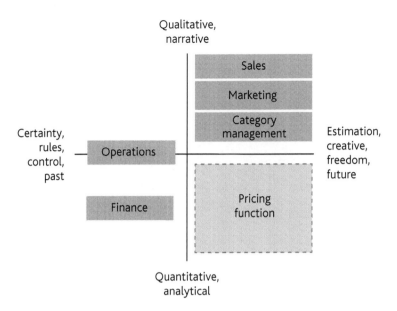

Figure 27 The orientation of business functions

The pricing function takes up a special position amidst that constellation, requiring a combination of orientations that is not found elsewhere in business operations. The art of pricing calls for a creative approach that focuses on the future, while the success of the science of pricing is driven by a quantitative and analytical approach. A better pricing policy is therefore conditional on a combination of both approaches. The pricing function comes somewhere in between the financial department and the commercial departments.

15.3 Deliverables and scope

The pricing function covers a broad territory, because prices are linked to aspects of the — external — demand side and the — internal — supply side. Despite that, the scope and deliverables of pricing are easy to describe.[*]

---

[*] Also refer to the description of the output of the pricing process in Chapter 13

Deliverables:
- gross prices, discounts, and net prices that customer pay, the pricing model (the basis for the price) and the commercial conditions with financial impact

Scope:
- activities and decisions that culminate in the setting of prices. This concerns decision-making processes and analysis with solid foundations, but also the execution, including price elements in processes such as sales, billing, and performance measurements and in systems such as CRM and ERP

These definitions are easy to grasp. The actual activities cover a broader range than many managers initially realize. Prices are deeply intertwined with financial and commercial processes. Ownership of the domain is not obtained in the short term. The correlation between price and financial and commercial results demands an open way of working, focused on collaboration with other departments. Pricing decisions can only be implemented successfully when they can count on broad support across the organization. Internally, the information needs to be transparent and clear. The pricing function has a great connecting role within the company.

In practice, pricing managers gradually acquire pricing authority, carefully aligning decisions with the business owner, normally the CEO of the company or business unit. Marginal propositions in the product and services portfolio, peripheral markets, or small stakes are low down on the list of priorities.

Performance measurement of the pricing process can be tackled through finance and controlling. Forecasting the effects of the policy on KPIs will make posterior interpretation of the results more meaningful.

15.4 The position of pricing in the organization

15.4.1 MANAGEMENT AND INITIATIVE

Running the pricing function from board level will bring focus, priority, and unity in the implementation of improvements. At smaller companies or a business unit, a pricing manager on the management team can take charge of the pricing function. At large multinationals, the role of Chief Pricing Officer (CPO) is specifically geared to that. The CPO leads the pricing initiative.

Under the direction of a Chief Pricing Officer, who is an independent member of the board, the function will have the room it needs to fulfill the potential of pricing. A CPO runs a small department of pricing experts who coordinate and take care of the art, science, and execution of pricing. The pricing function does its work independently, making objective and fact-based analyses regarding the company's commercial course. This status of "non-normative calculators" is precious.

15.4.2 THE ROLES OF CPO AND PRICING TEAM

The Chief Pricing Officer defines the revenue model and sets the pricing strategy (art). The CPO obtains input from strategists and commercial executives. He or she runs strategic decisions by other board members and business owners. These are the CEOs of the business units with P&L responsibility for part of the company. The CPO has a clear say in the selection of the business model and overarching corporate strategy.

The analysis of and decisions about the level of prices (science) are made in close consultation with higher echelons of management of the department that traditionally took the lead in pricing matters. The Chief Pricing Officer does so through a team of pricing managers and analysts that works closely together with commercial and financial managers, and that reports to the CEO of the corresponding business unit.

The CPO steers process experts toward optimum pricing process design. They compile requirements for IT systems and processes based on the functional management of pricing managers and the CPO. Project managers are responsible for process savings, resource substantiation, required improvements to information provision, and interfaces with other departments.

15.4.3 PRICING BOARD

Broad support at the top is indispensable. It is therefore often useful to set up a pricing board or program Steering Committee during the early years in the development of a conscious pricing function. This kind of stand-alone forum is made up of board members and a few senior managers from sales and finance.

The Steering Committee (SteerCo) will initiate and monitor projects and programs, make tough decisions about the set-up of the organization, and discuss delicate pricing decisions with major impact. These issues will be the subject of more detailed contemplation than the C-level is used to. This exclusive attention for and focus on pricing will kick-start a learning curve for individual members and the group as a whole alike.

15.4.4 COMPROMISE

Unfortunately, suitable candidates for the role of Chief Pricing Officer with sufficient pricing expertise and executive-level experience are hard to come by.

Today, in the year 2013, many a major corporation has added the CPO role to the portfolio of one of the board members, who is then supported by a global head of pricing. This is an important step in the development toward an optimum and independent pricing function. The existing "split" of pricing responsibilities among departments and board members has, however, largely remained intact. This makes that the focus on pricing is still suboptimal, while pricing efforts are not fully unified.

The head of pricing* generally reports to the head of the department that traditionally holds final responsibility for pricing. At retailers, this is the director of merchandising/category management, while at consumer goods manufacturers the marketing & sales director has pricing authority, and at B2B suppliers it can very well be the CFO. The department that outranks all others when it comes to pricing sometimes receives insufficient appreciation and trust from other departments: finance finds the sales department cavalier and overly revenue-driven, and sales sees finance as slow and bureaucratic. From the start, the pricing teams must build a reputation for objectivity, speed, and proactiveness. Only then will they be able to free themselves from existing perceptions. (Overly) negative perceptions of business functions are conducive to the next step toward a solution with an independent CPO coming into view sooner, as the pricing function will then not be held back by the past as much.

---

* Other job titles might be pricing VP or senior pricing manager

CHAPTER 16

Change

16.1 The first steps are the hardest

The first thing a CEO who has just been introduced to the importance of pricing does is often to "try something" and run a pilot project. The possibility of appointing a Chief Pricing Officer has not even been broached yet at that stage. The choice of such a trial project is important for the person taking the initiative for it. The results will determine the further course of the development of the pricing function. The power of price makes it easy to achieve positive results. And yet, pricing managers struggle to claim these results and preach pricing. That is down to the fact that the influence of the factor price is not unequivocally demonstrable. Efforts to isolate the unique influence of price are consequently key in the experiments that are part of the first forays into an independent pricing function.

For example, a profit boost of a hundred thousand euros through the implementation of a new revenue model at one major customer can significantly raise pricing's profile, even on a total turnover of 200 million euros. Both account manager and customer relate their experience with great enthusiasm, explaining why they are so pleased with the new revenue model and the pricing manager's work. This, in turn, convinces others across the organization; a forty-times greater profit boost of four million euros will sometimes be less eye-catching. With a 6% price increase on 40% of products and a 2% price cut on 20% of products, the unique impact of the price factor will be less notable due to simultaneous product portfolio changes, sales staff performance and market trends.

In the 20th century, it took new business functions such as HR, marketing, and IT decades to establish themselves. After it was first suggested that companies should do more to improve the quality of their workforce, it still took a long time for HR management to be introduced. And the appointment of a business-driven CIO came years after the advent of IT. Integration and optimization of pricing expertise in companies is therefore likely to remain an item on the agenda of boards of directors for years to come.

Pricing is an integral part of a company. After all, a commercial operation cannot sell services or products without prices. Despite that, the pricing *function* may remain an underrated process that unfolds in a company's subconscious, as HR, marketing, and IT were until well into the 20th century. Pricing capability's development to maturity requires a focus on the art, science, and execution of pricing.

This chapter will outline the change aspects that play a role in the development of a mature pricing function. The following section will first go into the change approach. Following that, we will discuss the enablers of change, such as information provision, tooling, and pricing resources.

16.2   Change approach

16.2.1   BEYOND THE AD-HOC APPROACH

The first serious pricing projects generally immediately reveal the power of a better pricing policy. And yet, managers often do not let that change their ad-hoc approach to pricing. Commercial managers or controllers take a pricing course and make some changes here and there. Pricing analysts perform activities with limited scope on the sidelines of the business. There is no progress on structure. Revenue models are still mostly chosen subconsciously, the power of most price drivers remains unknown, and structural knowledge of price sensitivity is lacking.

And companies that do want to take pricing further tend to underestimate the obstacles. Dropping the ad-hoc approach and building a stable pricing capability requires structural adoption of change management, as the implications affect all parts of the company and its surroundings. This section will focus on the steps toward a pricing capability with a clearly defined profile in the organization. We will roughly apply Kotter's[79] change approach to pricing.

16.2.2 URGENCY AND COALITION

Pilot projects highlight the importance of pricing. Together with experienced commercial and financial managers, pricing experts unearth the potential. A diagnosis of the current status is vital in that context. This diagnosis and aforementioned pilots make up the ammunition needed to forge a coalition of influential commercial and financial managers and board members. Actually embracing the initiative will bind the coalition together. The final goal will therefore continue to stand, even when faced with setbacks along the way.

16.2.3 VISION AND BUSINESS PLAN

Pilots and diagnoses are also the starting point for the formulation of a content-based vision of the pricing function, which is subsequently captured in the pricing business plan. This business plan defines the crucial changes, and covers the revenue model, strategy, deployment of tools, creation of a pricing department, set-up of processes, and determination of authorizations. The plan estimates the efficiency gains at existing departments brought by process optimization and presents the complete financial business case for the pricing initiative.[*]

---

[*] The pricing initiative normally achieves a very positive balance of income and expenditure

16.2.4 PROJECT GOVERNANCE

Governance is bestowed directly on the executive management team or board, or on a pricing Steering Committee for all projects. In the latter case both key board members and senior managers at the departments involved will be represented on the pricing SteerCo. This Committee has a clear mandate. The formulated vision and the business plan are the roadmap for the steering of the program. The SteerCo has formal and informal powers, and records decisions clearly and transparently. This Committee will have to overcome resistance from across the organization and clear obstacles.

16.2.5 COMMUNICATION

The pricing team and the line managers communicate the changes to the departments. That is a laborious task that requires considerable time and attention, which is not always readily available, because better prices in the business — the pricing manager's top priority — often have to be delivered fast. A welcome helping hand comes as middle managers who are indirectly involved in pricing are generally quick to recognize the point of having a pricing department: they are surprised that such a department doesn't already exist.

This may be different at the department that used to be the top authority for pricing matters. Its response might be: "but we're doing a fine job as it is". Getting the manager of this department to buy into the idea of a dedicated pricing team is then essential in helping get the value added by such a pricing team across and garnering sufficient support across the company.

16.2.6 CONSOLIDATION AND ANCHORING

Successes help consolidate changes and keep innovation on the agenda. That may sound trivial, but pricing managers sometimes see support for further innovation drop after they have registered the first successes and the attention of corporate executives shifts to other challenges or fashionable strategic topics.

Anchoring pricing in corporate culture is another focus point. B2B suppliers, for example, can improve pricing merely by analyzing markets, customers, and win ratios. If they, however, keep rewarding sales staff based on the revenue they generate, they will perpetuate the sales force culture that comes with that. Rewarding them based on the margins they achieve will open up ways of further improving pricing and providing customers with better solutions.

Tools, information management, training, and resources are powerful instruments for anchoring. In the next section we will go into these enablers of pricing in greater detail.

16.3   Enablers of change

16.3.1   AVAILABILITY OF INFORMATION

The information that pricing needs as input is diverse and extensive. Price is a one-figure summary of what a company has to offer. The required information therefore comes from nearly every single part of the company, and can concern, among other things, markets, customers, and costs. Commercial departments generally have research findings about customers and markets that may prove useful input for the pricing effort.[*] Cost information is spread out over various departments. The required cross-sections of this data cannot be derived directly from the books. In deploying price drivers, a pricing manager will distinguish between price drivers based on the nature of the costs (fixed/variable, direct/indirect) and the development of costs over time.[†] There are more focus areas besides cost, customer, and market. Product strategy and development of innovations provide an idea of pricing opportunities, but the proportions of stakes in joint ventures, for example, may also be important.

---

[*] Refer to Part II, the second layer of implicit measurement of the FPF
[†] Refer to Part I

In practice, it is hard to gain quick access to all relevant data, even when it is already available at the company. Departments are not always quick to cooperate. Or they have not stored the information correctly and go on the defensive when they get a request for access to that information. The question "what do you need it for?" is one that will sound familiar to many a pricing manager.

It is impossible to predict exactly what information is available, which departments will cooperate promptly, and where you will come up against resistance. A convincing explanation of the significance of the information is required, as well as unequivocal and unconditional backing from the board.

16.3.2 EXAMPLE: OVERCOMING RESISTANCE

The pricing team at a service provider's sales department intends to make a detailed analysis of why certain tenders are successful and others are not. They want to compare the role of the price to the impact of other value drivers. The pricing manager therefore asks bid management for all the information it has about tenders, RFPs, and feedback from customers from the past years. Due to the administrative side of its work and internal politics, bid management comes under the finance department. As it turns out, the department has not filed past tenders properly. The head of the department does not want that to come out, and therefore denies the pricing team access to the data.

After an intervention by the board, the pricing team does eventually get hold of the details it needs. The data is delivered in a bit of a mess, in separate files on CDs that contain many gigabytes of information. The pricing team spends weeks trudging through the information on the CDs, structuring data from tenders, text documents, and emails into a value performance database. The subsequent analyses of the causes of success and failure of tenders eventually reveal the influence of price.

The win ratio in tender processes originally hovered around the 30% mark. Using newly acquired pricing intelligence and a method of better responding to customer requirements, the pricing team manages to raise the win ratio to 45%, with profit margins staying the same.

Following this feat, bid management's administration was reorganized by its new head to be completely as per the pricing team's requirements. Both the CFO and the CCO have trusted the pricing managers' fact-based analyses blindly in their transactions ever since.

16.3.3 SUPPORT FROM IT

The IT department plays a big part in ensuring access to information and deployment of the FPF for pricing science. It rolls out financial and marketing tools with insights that are relevant to pricing, such as profitability per customer, product offering, and market shares. Sometimes a special request is required, for example for an SQL query that collates data from separate sources, which can be used to identify correlations. IT routinely complies with such requests from across the company, providing it gets the background information it needs.

There are cases where, after explanation of the priority of and reasons behind the request, IT staff is adamant that it is impossible to build the requested solution, much to the surprise of the pricing manager, who has a description of data tables to underpin the request. This misalignment of opinions is often down to data quality. Most software packages are, in fact, not used to their full potential. Suboptimal use of a CRM system, for example, whereby users save duplicate drafts of customer proposals under consideration or the system does not record customer responses to sales quotes, leads to poor registration of price negotiation processes. A new protocol for users could in such cases improve the quality of the data. Support from the users' line management is an essential prerequisite for that.

Another cause may be that IT's demands for data quality exceed the quality level needed to be able to run a pricing analysis. That is because price research focuses on correlations. A pricing manager can produce meaningful results using only the part of the data that is of good quality.

In the long term, collaboration with IT can be optimized by gradually introducing improvements. Their expertise will, over time, earn pricing managers better access to data and more privileges. They will be manning the front line in the battle for big data fought by CIOs. Formal endorsement by the board will speed up this development.

16.3.4 PRICING TOOLS AND SOFTWARE

Effective tools will secure quality of the execution. Here too, a step-by-step approach will yield the best results. Pricing managers are best off testing new tools or functionality on a modest scale first. They will achieve fine initial results using only spreadsheets, databases, or statistical programs and BI*/query tools† on ERP, CRM, and data warehouse‡ systems. These programs and systems are used by most companies as standard, and they are managed by the IT department.

Success will prompt a broad rollout of the method. The pricing team will then compile documentation for training and support. Pricing analysts or IT analysts will design a structural and stable analysis model based on the pilot and a data quality diagnosis. IT, in turn, will computerize and standardize the method for widespread rollout using existing BI tools and CRM or ERP systems.

In-house development of tools with features tailored to a company's own business, while also being compatible with existing systems and processes, does not have to take long. Examples include a calculation model to break down the financial implications of deals, analysis programs for structural use of value drivers in the optimization of price lists, a waterfall chart of types of discount, a performance measurement of past price changes, or reports about competitors' prices.

In case of long-term or large-scale use, the pricing team will, together with the IT department, look into whether procurement of third-party software would be beneficial in terms of efficiency or effec-

* BI: Business Intelligence
† Query tools: these are tools that enable retrieval of specific data and reports from a database
‡ Data warehouse: databases built for analyses, containing data from a range of different business systems, whereby the definition of the data will be mutually aligned as much as possible

tiveness. Formulation of business requirements based on successful pilots is the first and most important step. Only then will it be meaningful to compare the functionality offered by the software vendors to the requirements. In doing so, IT and pricing managers will offset the costs and benefits of third-party software against further in-house development of tools.

16.3.5 HUMAN RESOURCES

Demands made on a pricing manager are high. He or she must possess a rare combination of commercial and strategic qualities and analytical skills.

Building a career in price management, as is done in marketing, sales, or finance, is still an uncommon phenomenon. Pricing managers are highly visible in a company. If successful, they move into other commercial or financial roles in the higher echelons of companies relatively quickly.

Recruiters are not (yet) adept at recruiting pricing resources, and experienced candidates are often not available in the labor market due to the rapid growth of the pricing discipline. Retraining internal staff for pricing roles is therefore a good way of supplementing external recruitment.

The pricing team must be made up of a combination of seasoned pros from sales and marketing and talents from finance. It can then right from the start rely on an effective blend of skills, experiences, and, last but not least, understanding of the company. That way, the pricing team can quickly pick up enough speed and take pricing to a higher level, because the team members have got the lay of the land and understand how markets and customers respond.

When internal communication is good, commercial and financial managers will accept and embrace the high return on pricing expertise. The pricing team then becomes the natural home in the company for the "box of tricks" that is pricing. Pricing managers are a mainstay in the decision-making about the commercial strategy.

16.3.6 TRAINING

A pricing team harnesses specific pricing skills and develops these further. To that end, it designs its own internal training programs. Knowledge transfer occurs through peer-to-peer support and review. Internal business-specific training options are an effective resource in anchoring knowledge in the organization. Detailed documentation about the working method for pricing employees and more general explanations for commercial and financial staff are only powerful tools when they are tailored to the company, its markets, and its processes.

Training courses are easy to develop during the early stage of the building of a pricing function. After all, the rollout of tools, methods, and process set-ups will over the years always go hand in hand with careful implementation. Commercial or financial employees involved must be given the details of the underlying reasons for changes. Together with high-level conceptual board presentations about progress and strategy, this kind of training forms the core of the instructional material for new employees.

16.3.7 INCENTIVES AND TARGETS

Incentives and targets are used by the management of a company to steer behavior in a certain direction and allow staff leeway in putting policy into practice. Commercial staff will then not be restricted by a proliferation of guidelines. Self-interest will steer them in the right direction. Bonus mechanisms stimulate managers' entrepreneurial spirit and creativity and will help them go that extra mile to land clients.

Incentives often heighten sales staff's focus on revenue. The inherent motivation to land a client is intensified by revenue-related targets. However, revenue-based remuneration is less suited in the case of pricing managers. A one-sided emphasis on raising revenue, through a price cut, for example, is bound to put a strain on profits. This would be an undesirable situation.

A pricing team would fare much better with the kind of remuneration structure that is used for financial managers and board members. Their targets are aligned with strategic objectives, such as margins and profitability, or the value of the company.

Notes

1   K. Mitchell, "The next frontier of the pricing profession", in A. Hinterhuber, S. Liozu, *Innovation in Pricing*, Routledge (2013) [p. 403-409]

2   A. Lashinsky, *Inside Apple — The Secrets Behind the Past and Future Success of Steve Jobs's Iconic Brand*, John Murray (2012) and W. Isaacson, *Steve Jobs: The Exclusive Biography*, Little Brown Book Group (2011)

3   R.S. Tedlow, "Sam Walton: Great From the Start". *Working Knowledge,* Harvard Business School (July 23rd, 2001, retrieved May 17th, 2012)

4   J.L. de Jager, *De memoires van een optimist*, de Prom (1997)

5   M.V. Marn, R.L. Rosiello, "Managing Price, Gaining Profit", *Harvard Business Review*, [p. 84-94] (Sep-Oct 1992), M.V. Marn, E.V. Roegner, C.C. Zawada, *The Price Advantage*, John Wiley & Sons (2004)

6   P. Winsemius, *Je gaat het pas zien, als je het doorhebt*, Balans Uitgeverij (2004) (title is a well-known statement by Johan Cruijff)

7   V.R. Rao, B. Kartono, "Pricing objectives and strategies: a cross-country survey", in: V.R. Rao, *Handbook of pricing research in marketing*, Edward Elgar Publishing (2009) [p. 9-35], S. M. Liozu, A. Hinterhuber, R. Boland, S. Perelli, "The conceptualization of value based pricing in industrial firms", *Journal of Revenue and Pricing Management* (2012), A. Blinder, E. Canetti, D. Lebow, J. Rudd, *Asking About Prices: A New Approach to Understanding Price Stickiness*, Russell Sage Foundation (1998)

8   Refer to, for example, T.T. Nagle, R.K. Holden, *The Strategy And Tactics Of Pricing*, Prentice Hall (1987), R.J. Dolan, H. Simon, *Power Pricing*, Free Press (1997), E. Mitchell, *Profitable pricing strategies*, Alexander Hamilton Institute (1985), R. Dolan, "How do you know when the price is right?", *Harvard Business Review* (Sep-Oct 1995), R. Mohammed, *The art of pricing — how to find the hidden profits to grow your business*, Crown business (2005), S. M. Liozu, A. Hinterhuber, R. Boland, S. Perelli, "The conceptualization of value based pricing in industrial firms", *Journal of Revenue and Pricing Management* (2012)

9   A J. Raju, Z.J. Zhang, *Smart Pricing*, Wharton School Publishing (April 2010)

10 Refer to, for example, J. Dijksma, *Kosten — Inleiding tot de bedrijfseconomische kostenvraagstukken*, Wolters-Noordhoff (1988) and J. Dijksma, *Vraagstukken over*

bedrijfseconomische winst- en vermogensbepaling, Wolters-Noordhoff (1985) or other introductory textbooks on cost management

11   A.J. Raju, Z.J. Zhang, *Smart Pricing*, Wharton School Publishing (2010)

12   Visit to Albert Heijn supermarket, Breukelen, and website, www.ah.nl, consulted on August 24th (2012)

13   Visit to Albert Heijn supermarket, Breukelen, and website, www.ah.nl, consulted on July 20th (2012)

14   Refer to reports in the media, such as: A. Wokke, "2010: providers draaien de klok terug", www.tweakers.net, consulted on December 20th (2010) and D. Reijerman, "Mobiel bellen duurder geworden door afrekenen per minuut", www.tweakers.net, consulted on March 6th (2010)

15   E. Porter, *Alles heeft een prijs* (2011), translation of: *The Price of Everything*, Portfolio Penguin (2011)

16   *The Economist*, "The price of information", www.economist.com, 4 February (2012) and *The Guardian*, "Harvard University says it can't afford journal publishers' prices", www.guardian.co.uk, April 24th (2012)

17   K. Anderson, "Have Journal Prices Really Increased Much in the Digital Age?", scholarlykitchen.sspnet.org, January 8th (2013)

18   F.F. Bilstein, F. Luby, H. Simon, *Manage for profit not for market share*, Harvard Business School Press (2006)

19   Ibid.

20   R. Oever, "Ahold: Polderaar in het nauw", *FEM Business*, No. 44 (2006) and other publications in the media

21   Refer to, for example, T.T. Nagle, R.K. Holden, *The Strategy And Tactics Of Pricing*, Prentice Hall (1987), R.J. Dolan, H. Simon, *Power Pricing*, Free Press (1997)

22   T.T. Nagle, R.K. Holden, *The Strategy And Tactics Of Pricing*, Prentice Hall (3rd edition, 2002)

23   R. Leszinski, M.V. Marn, "Setting Value, not Price", *McKinsey Quarterly*, Nr 1 (1997) [p98-115], M.V. Marn, E.V. Roegner, C.C. Zawada, *The Price Advantage*, John Wiley & Sons (2004)

24   R.J. Dolan, H. Simon, *Power Pricing*, Free Press (1997)

25   S.E. Prokesch, "Competing on Customer Service", *Harvard Business Review* (Nov-Dec 1995) [p. 100-118]

26   J.M. Meehan, M.G. Simonetto, L. Montan, C.A. Goodin, *Pricing and Profitability Management — a practical guide for business leaders*, John Wiley & Sons (Asia) (2011)

27   W. Isaacson, *Steve Jobs: The Exclusive Biography*, Little Brown Book Group (2011)

28   E. Ben-Yosef, *The Evolution of the U.S. Airline Industry: Theory, Strategy and Policy*, Springer (2005)

29   Ibid.

30   A. Lashinsky, *Inside Apple — The Secrets Behind the Past and Future Success of Steve Jobs's Iconic Brand*, John Murray (2012) and W. Isaacson, *Steve Jobs: The Exclusive Biography*, Little Brown Book Group (2011)

31   W. Poundstone, *Priceless: the Myth of Fair Value (and how to take advantage of it)*, Hill and Wang (2010)

32   Ibid.

33   NS website, ns.nl, consulted on February 13th (2012)

34   D. Ariely, *Predictably Irrational*, Harper (2009)

35   S. Plous, *The Psychology of Judgment and Decision Making*, McGraw-Hill (1993)

36   Ibid.

37   W. Poundstone, *Priceless: the Myth of Fair Value (and how to take advantage of it)*, Hill and Wang (2010)

38   Ibid.

39   D. Ariely, *Predictably Irrational*, Harper (2009)

40   W. Poundstone, *Priceless: the Myth of Fair Value (and how to take advantage of it)*, Hill and Wang (2010)

41   P. Underhill, *Waarom we kopen, wat we kopen*, Forum (1999) (*Why we buy, The science of shopping*, Simon & Schuster)

42   Albert Heijn website, www.ah.nl, December 2nd (2012)

43   P. de W. Wijnen, "Prijsaanpassingen Albert Heijn vooral omhoog", *NRC Handelsblad*, October 19th (2011)

44   P. Smit, "Site waakt over AH-prijzen", *Distrifood*, consulted on 11 December (2010)

45   R.B. McKenzie, *Why Popcorn Costs So Much at the Movies*, Springer (2008), C. Balan, "Research on Odd Prices — Dead end of field of potential innovation", in A. Hinterhuber, S.Liozu, *Innovation in Pricing*, Routledge (2013) [p. 376-392]

46   J. Tirole, *The Theory of Industrial Organization*, The MIT Press (1988)

47   H.T. Pijl, "Prijsontwikkeling op de Nederlandse benzinemarkt", De Nederlandsche Bank, www.dnb.nl (2002)

48   Ibid.

49   H. van Gelder, X. van Uffelen, "Zeven meter papier over de benzinemarkt", *de Volkskrant*, July 4th (2002)

50   Nu.nl, "Benzinemarkt werkt naar behoren", www.nu.nl based on ANP, November 1st (2011)

51   E.E.C. van Damme, "Pompen of verzuipen", *ESB*, no. 4354 (2002)

52   M. Levine, "Airline Competition in Deregulated Markets: Theory, Firm Strategy and Public Policy", *Yale Journal on Regulation*, 4 (1987) [p393-494]

53   Schuttevaer.nl, "EVO: Gefronste wenkbrauwen verladers na tariefstijging containervaart", www.schuttevaer.nl, February 3rd (2012)

54   J. Raju, Z.J. Zhang, *Smart Pricing*, Wharton School Publishing (2010)

55   Dell website, www.dell.nl, consulted on February 20th (2012)

56   Apple website, store.apple.com/nl, consulted on February 20th (2012)

57   C. Anderson, *Free — The Future of a Radical Price*, Random House Business Books (2009), Wikipedia, nl.wikipedia.org/wiki/ King_Camp_ Gillette, consulted on February 27th (2012)

58   Electronica.infonu.nl, electronica.infonu.nl/huishoudelijk/42405-senseo-nespresso-of-toch-de-espressomachine.html, February 27th (2012)

59   Nespresso, www.nespresso.com/#/nl/nl/coffee_nespresso, consulted on November 1st (2012)

60   Conversation with sales assistant, Nespresso store P.C. Hooftstraat, Amsterdam, March 4th (2011)

61   J. Jarvis, *What Would Google Do?*, HarperBusiness (2009)

62   W. Poundstone, *Priceless: the Myth of Fair Value (and how to take advantage of it)*, Hill and Wang (2010)

63   P.S. Dempsey, "The financial performance of the airline industry post-deregulation", *Houston Law Review*, no. 2, Vol 45 (2008) [p. 421-485]

64   J.C. Anderson, N. Kumar, J.A. Narus, *Value Merchants — Demonstrating and documenting superior value in business markets*, Harvard Business School Press (2007)

65   For decision-making processes at customer, refer to: S. E. Heiman, D. Sanchez, T. Tuleja, *The New Strategic Selling*, First Warner Books Printing (1998)

66   For an academic overview, refer to: K. Jedidi, S. Jagpal, "Willingness to pay: measurement and managerial implications", in: V.R. Rao, *Handbook of pricing research in marketing*, Edward Elgar Publishing (2009) [p. 37-60]

67   J. Stewart, *Econometrics*, Philip Allan (1991), G.S. Maddala, *Limited Dependent and Qualitative Variables in Econometrics*, Cambridge University Press (1983)

68   P.H. Franses, R. Paap, *Quantitative models in marketing research*, Cambridge University Press (2001)

69   P. de Pelsmacker, P van Kenhove, *Marktonderzoek*, Garant (1999)

70   T. Stewart, "Growth as a Process — An Interview with Jeffrey Immelt CEO GE", *Harvard Business Review*, June (2006)

71   S. Liozu, K. Ecker, "The Organizational Design of the Pricing Function in Firms", in A. Hinterhuber, S.Liozu, *Innovation in Pricing*, Routledge (2013) [p. 27-45]

72   A. Smith, *An Inquiry into the Nature and Causes of the Wealth of Nations*, W. Strahan and T. Cadell (1776). Adam Smith introduced the term "the invisible hand" of the market that defines the market price based on supply and demand

73   D. Jaffee, *Organization Theory — Tension and Change*, McGraw-Hill Education (2008)

74   W. Crouch, G. Hunsicker, "The Journey to Pricing Excellence — The case of a mid-sized manufacturing firm", in A. Hinterhuber, S.Liozu, *Innovation in Pricing*, Routledge (2013) [p. 178-182]

75   D. Ariely, *Predictably Irrational*, Harper (2009)

76   Also refer to M.V. Marn, E.V. Roegner, C.C. Zawada, *The Price Advantage*, John Wiley & Sons (2004)

77   P. Kotler, G. Armstrong, *Principles of Marketing*, Prentice Hall (1989) [4th edition]

78   Vodafone, vodafone.nl, consulted on October 27th (2012)

79   J.P. Kotter, *Leading Change*, Harvard Business School Press (1996) [1st edition]

Index

Made in the USA
Lexington, KY
07 January 2015